CHILDREN OF POVERTY

Studies on the Effects of Single Parenthood, the Feminization of Poverty, and Homelessness

edited by

STUART BRUCHEY
University of Maine

A GARLAND SERIES

IMPROVING CHILDREN'S LIVES

ALTERNATIVES TO CURRENT ANTIPOVERTY POLICY

REBECCA Y. KIM

GARLAND PUBLISHING, Inc.
NEW YORK & LONDON / 1996

Library of Congress Cataloging-in-Publication Data

Kim, Rebecca Y., 1957–
    Improving children's lives : alternatives to current antipov-
erty policy / Rebecca Y. Kim.
        p.   cm. — (Children of poverty)
    Includes bibliographical references and index.
    ISBN 0-8153-2538-X (alk. paper)
    1. Public welfare—United States. 2. Child welfare—United
States. 3. Poor children—United States. 4. Family allowances—
United States. 5. Income maintenance programs—United States.
I. Title. II. Series.
HV95.K45 1996
362.7'0973—dc20   96-36706

Printed on acid-free, 250-year-life paper
Manufactured in the United States of America

Contents

Tables

Preface

For the last three decades, the public income transfer system for families with children in the United States has been criticized for being overly targeted on extremely poor families headed by single mothers. Most criticism has focused on two features of the system: its categorical nature and its reliance on income-tested benefits. Categorical requirements for eligibility, which limit benefits mainly to single-parent families, have been criticized as unfair to two-parent families and as discouraging marriage. Income-tested benefits have been reprimanded because they discourage work in that they reduce benefits by extremely high rates as earnings increase.

To remedy these shortcomings of the over-targeted system, the author discusses three policy proposals, all providing universal benefits: (1) a refundable tax credit for children; (2) universal health care coverage; and (3) a child support assurance system.

In analyzing the three policy changes, the author estimates what benefits would result at what cost using the 1987 panel of Survey of Income and Program Participation. Of particular interest are the potential interaction effects that would result when the three universal programs are combined as a package. Although previous research has provided estimates of the benefits and costs of particular universal programs, this study is the first to address the question of whether the economic effect of the combined programs is equal to the sum of the single programs' effects performed alone or greater than the sum.

The findings indicate that the impact of the programs interacting with one another would far exceed the sum of the impacts produced by each program alone. In other words, a multi-faceted approach becomes much more effective in both reducing poverty incidence among children and inducing AFDC families to work and move off welfare. Finally, the author concludes that the United States needs to redirect public policy for families with children from the income-tested (welfare) to non-income-tested (universal) approach.

This study is indebted to Dr. Irwin Garfinkel, major professor of my dissertation committee. Not only has he funded the study, but also he has given me many hours of intensive discussion and excellent perspectives on this work. My special thanks go to Dr. Daniel R.

Meyer, committee member, for his tremendous support and numerous insightful comments from the very beginning of the study. Without his patient help for micro-simulation programming, this analysis would have been impossible. I also appreciate suggestions and comments given by other committee members Drs. Barbara Wolfe, Robert Haveman, and Irving Piliavin. Despite my appreciation of these individuals, I am alone responsible for any errors made in the final product of this study.

Improving Children's Lives

I

Introduction

Concerns about children in the United States have increased in the past decades. Many studies have shown that U.S. children are considerably worse off than the elderly in this country--one of the most vulnerable groups--and than children in other industrial countries.[1] In particular, major changes in family structure over the past decades have affected unfavorably the well-being and futures of children. Research has found that the increasing occurrence of marital break-ups and out-of-wedlock births have contributed to a deterioration in the economic well-being of children. The poor conditions in which today's children live are drawing a renewed interest in the public transfer programs intended to assist them.

Under the current system, the major income transfer programs for poor families with children are Aid to Families with Dependent Children (AFDC), food stamps, Medicaid, and private child support from an absent parent. However, the current system has been criticized on many grounds: for its work-disincentive effect and resulting "welfare trap"; for causing marital break-ups; as being an inequitable benefit system; as being administratively costly; and for stigmatizing recipients (Garfinkel, 1982). Although most people recognize that the government should assure some minimum level of existence for families with children, how that should be accomplished has been a subject of considerable debate during the past decades. One of the most critical issues in this debate has been whether or not benefits should be income-tested. The issue often involves two conflicting goals: improving the economic condition of these children or reducing their families' dependence on public support. Policy choices among alternative approaches to income transfer, thus, imply trade-offs between certain benefits and costs associated with each approach. Since the current income transfer system for families with children is mainly characterized by income-tested programs, the benefits and costs of non-income-tested programs as an alternative approach is an interesting

3

policy question: a measure of the relative performance of this alternative could provide a rationale for policy making. The purpose of this study is to estimate the economic effects of a combined program of non-income-tested transfers such as child support assurance, children's allowance, and universal health coverage.

PROFILE OF FAMILIES WITH CHILDREN IN THE UNITED STATES

Demographic Trends

The most astonishing change over the past two decades has occurred in family structure where children live. The number of single-parent families with children has increased rapidly during this period. This trend is largely the result of higher divorce rates, lower remarriage rates, and an increase in the number of never-married mothers. Between 1950 and 1981, the divorce rate more than doubled (Bianchi, 1990). Since 1981, the divorce rate has levelled off but still remains high, at a rate of 4.8 per 1000 of the population in 1988 (Green Book, 1991, p.950). In addition, there has been a significant increase in the number of births to unmarried mothers. In 1988, one in four children born in the Unites States was to an unmarried mother, up from only 1 in 20 children born in 1960 (Green Book, 1991, p.950). Among blacks, more than three out of every five children were born out of wedlock (Green Book, 1991, p.950).

The changing composition of families has directly affected the living arrangements of children. The number of children in two-parent families has declined. In 1989, 73% of all children under the age of 18 were living in two-parent families, whereas they accounted for 88% in 1960 (U.S. Bureau of the Census, 1989, Table 4). The prevalence of single-parent families is especially noticeable among black children: 55% of all black children under age 18 lived with one parent in 1989 (U.S. Bureau of the Census, 1989, p.953). Also, among children in single-parent families, the majority (almost 90%) lived with a mother rather than a father.

Taking a cross-sectional percentage of children living in single-parent families understates the incidence of single parenthood for children, because parents change marital status over time as children grow up. Some studies have estimated that about 42% of all white children and about 86% of all black children born in the late 1970s lived some time in mother-only families before they reached the age of 18 (see Bumpass, 1984; Hofferth, 1985). Also, Garfinkel and McLanahan (1986) indicates that the median length of time spent in single motherhood is about six years, indicating that most children spend a third of childhood time in such families (p. 47). This reflects that the single-parent family is a common experience in the lives of today's children.

Poverty Among Children

In the past several years, much attention has been focused on the declining poverty rates of the elderly and the growing poverty among children. Today, more than one out of every five children are living below the official poverty line, and 40% of all the poor are children. For some demographic groups, child poverty is more severe: in 1991, 46% of all black children and 40% of all Hispanic children were in official poverty; among children under the age of 6, almost one-quarter are poor; and among children living in mother-only families, more than half are in poverty.[2]

A comparative framework, as suggested by Corbett (1993), can provide a good indicator of the economic status of children in this country. Looking at a change in poverty rates over time, poverty among children has been on the rise during much of the last two decades. Although poverty for children under the age of 18 declined significantly between 1960 and 1970, from 26.5% to 14.9%, it has increased steadily afterwards to 17.9% in 1980 and to 19.9% in 1990 (Danziger and Weinberg, 1992, Table 4). These over-time rates of poverty illustrate that the poverty incidence among children has increased by one-third over the past two decades. They also imply that the rate of poverty for children has risen by an average of about one percentage point every four years.

We can also compare poverty rates among different population groups. According to Corbett (1993), "a child in 1991 was twice as likely to be poor as a prime-age adult and almost twice as likely to be poor as an elderly person" (p.2). He also indicated that the poverty rate for all elderly people (12.4% in 1991), one of the most vulnerable groups, is now less than the overall national average of 14.2%. This positive progress against poverty among the elderly contrasts with the deteriorating trend in poverty among children over the same time. International comparisons, finally, show the most disturbing picture. The U.S. poverty rate among children is "more than twice that of the United Kingdom and Canada, four times the French rate, and over ten times the Swedish rate" (Corbett, 1993, p.2). These international comparisons highlight that child poverty is more widespread in the United States than in any other industrialized nation.

Why are children poor? What accounts for their poor economic situation? Garfinkel and McLanahan (1986) have suggested several factors, including the increased number of families headed by women; lack of child support from absent parents; low earnings capacity of parent(s); and a decline in the value of transfer benefits available to low-income families.[3] The most frequently mentioned cause of child poverty is a change in family structure. Some studies indicate that changes in family structure cause the most poverty among female-headed families with children. Bane and Ellwood (1986), for example, indicate that the transition to a female-headed family is the most important event for falling into poverty, accounting for 59% of cases.

The importance of marital disruption or nonmarital births as a major factor affecting the poverty incidence of children living in female-headed families raises the issue of child support from the absent father. Many studies have showed that their economic difficulties arise as a result of unequal parental obligation.[4] Under the current child support system, most noncustodial fathers do not pay a reasonable amount of child support (Garfinkel and McLanahan, 1986). Indeed, national data on child support indicate the very low level of child support contribution from absent fathers: in 1989, only about 58% of the children who were potentially eligible for child support received an award. Of those with awards, only 44% received the full amount due, but nearly a quarter received no payment at all. Of those who pay, the child support amounts received are too low and represent a small portion of the single mother's income. Child support payments from absent father account for about 19% of the income of single white mothers and for 16% of the income of single black mothers (U.S. Bureau of the Census, 1990 (June), Table C).

Another cause of poverty for children living in female-headed families is the low earnings capacity of the mother (Garfinkel and McLanahan, 1986). Since a single mother becomes the primary provider in her family when she is divorced or separated, the earnings capacity of mothers is the most important factor for their economic status. However, "female breadwinners earn only 35% as much as fathers in two-parent families, because of differences in labor force participation and wages" (Garfinkel and McLanahan, 1986, p.22). Compared with their male counterparts, women are less likely to have received on-the-job training. In addition, mothers are more likely to have discontinued their work often because of child care. These factors can contribute to their low earning capacity.

Finally, the relatively low public transfer benefits provided to families with children are often designated as a cause of poverty (Garfinkel and McLanahan, 1986). Research has indicated that only 17% of all pretransfer poor children were taken out of poverty due to transfers, which sharply contrasts with 77% for the elderly (Danziger, 1989). This implies that current public transfers do little for most poor children. (More about public transfers will be discussed later in this chapter.)

Children's Health Status and Insurance Coverage

Americans are currently spending more than 12% of the GNP for their health care (Katharine et al., 1991), which ranks as the highest proportion of national GNP in the world (Sardell, 1990, p.272). By contrast, health indicators of U.S. children are not prominent. The rate of infant mortality in the United States was the highest of 22 other industrial nations in 1991, at 8.9 per 1,000 births (National Commission to Prevent Infant Mortality [NCPIM], 1992). Approximately 7% of babies in the United States are born at low birth weight, which is higher than the rate in 30 other countries (NCPIM, 1992). Immunization rates for preschool children in the United States are also low. Fewer than 70% of white children and less than half of black children 1 to 4 years of age received immunizations against common childhood diseases in 1985 (U.S. Bureau of the Census, 1987, p.106).

Health care coverage could greatly affect children's health status. Health insurance for children in the United States is usually provided as dependents under the employer health insurance plans of their parent(s), under self-purchased plans, or under Medicaid. In 1989, 63% of all children were covered under employer-provided insurance, 10.5% under self-purchased nongroup insurance, and 19.6% under public programs (Sheils and Wolfe, 1992, p.122). Among pregnant women, about 60% were covered under employer-related insurance, either as employees or as dependent spouses; about 6% had self-purchased coverage; and 25% were covered under public programs (Sheils and Wolfe, 1992, p.122).

Under the current system of health care, however, many children and pregnant women remain left out of health care protection. Almost one out of every four children (23%) under age 18 were without health insurance at some time in 1987 (Monheit and Cunningham, 1992, p.158); and 14.4% of pregnant women were without health insurance in 1989 (National Commission on Children, 1991). In addition, children constitute a considerable percentage of the uninsured population. Among all 35 million uninsured individuals, children currently account for 33% (Center for National Health Program Studies, 1992, p.6). Moreover, during the past decade, the percentage of children under age 18 who were covered by private or public health insurance declined substantially. Monheit and Cunningham (1992) indicate that the percent of children uninsured for the full year increased by 40% between 1977 and 1987--from 12.7% to 17.8%--or by 3.1 million children (p.156). According to these authors, this increase in the number of uninsured children mainly resulted from the decline in the percentage covered by private, largely employment-related, coverage,[5] and the fact that fewer children in single-parent families were eligible for Medicaid due to retrenchment of AFDC.

Children's health coverage is strongly related to the poverty status of their parents. Among children in families with income below the poverty level, 45% were without insurance coverage for at least part of 1987 (a rate twice higher than that of all children), including nearly 25% who did not have coverage all year (Monheit and Cunningham, 1992, p.158). During the same year, Medicaid covered only less than one third of poor children all year (Monheit and Cunningham, 1992, p.158).

Health insurance coverage of a child is also strongly associated with family structure and his/her parent(s) working status. Monheit and

Cunningham (1992) indicate that children in two-parent families, especially those in which both parents are employed all year, have the lowest likelihood of being uninsured--less than 10%. On the other hand, children with single parents who fail to work all year, and children in two parents families where parents worked only part of the year are the most vulnerable groups, more likely to be uninsured than children with parent(s) not employed at all. 54% of children in two-parent families where parents were employed part of the year (higher than the 40% for neither parent being employed at all) and 41% of children with single-parents who worked part year (also higher than the 22% where a parent did not work the full year) were uninsured at some time in 1987 (Monheit and Cunningham, 1992, p.158). These higher rates arise because Medicaid provides health care coverage for children with nonworking parents. This indicates that the lack of access to health care among children is the most serious for those living with working but still poor parents.

The lack of insurance coverage among children particularly limits access to health care. It has been documented that, compared to children with either private or public insurance, uninsured children are less likely to have a usual source of care and have fewer physician visits for particular acute illnesses (Monheit and Cunningham, 1992, p.159). Uninsured children are also less likely to be adequately immunized than children with health insurance (Monheit and Cunningham, 1992, p.163). The inadequate health care system in this country helps explain why U.S. children are less healthy than those in other industrial countries.

Current Public Transfers

Major federal transfer programs to assist poor families with children include Aid to Families with Dependent Children (AFDC), food stamps, Medicaid, and Earned Income Tax Credits. The AFDC program provides major cash assistance to needy children, primarily those of poor single mothers, but also of incapacitated and some unemployed parents. The AFDC program is jointly operated by the federal and state governments: the federal government contributes a substantial portion (more than half) of the total AFDC expenditures; and administration of the program is delegated to the states within broad federal guidelines. More important, the states have the responsibility for determining eligibility standards and benefit levels. States establish their own need standards, define income and resource limits, and set benefit levels. As a consequence, maximum AFDC payments vary radically from state to state: for a three-person family, they ranged from $118 in Alabama to $779 in Alaska in 1988 (Green Book, 1989, p.539). In the aggregate level during the year, the AFDC program aided 3.7 million families including 7.3 million children (nearly one child in every nine), with AFDC benefits totalling $17 billion (Levitan, 1990, p.49).

The food stamp program has been established to ensure that the poor obtain basic dietary needs.[6] For eligibility, the program has financial, categorical, and employment/training-related tests. Its financial tests require that those eligible have monthly income and liquid assets below limits set by food stamp law. Under the employment/training-related tests, certain household members must register for work, accept suitable job offers, and fulfill work or training requirements established by state welfare agencies. Categorical eligibility rules make public assistance recipients (most AFDC and SSI recipients) automatically eligible for food stamps. For benefit levels, households receive a monthly allotment of food stamps based on their income and household size. In 1988, the maximum monthly food stamp allotment for a family of three was $236 (Green Book, 1989, p.1115). This amount is reduced by 30% of a household's net income after specified allowable deductions,[7] assuming a family spends 30% of its income on food. Among food stamp recipients in 1988, monthly benefits averaged $130 per household (Green Book, 1989, p.1114). In the aggregate level, a monthly average of 5.8 million households participated in the program at a benefit expenditure of about $12 billion (Green Book, 1990, p.1252 & p.1256). Among all food stamp recipient households, families with children constituted 61% (Green Book, 1990, p.1267), and half were female-headed families with children (Green Book, 1991, p.1399). Although AFDC families are automatically eligible for food stamps, only 85% received them (Green Book, 1990, p.1252), probably because of the program's stigma effect.

Medicaid is the federal government's most important health care program for the poor.[8] Since Medicaid provides health care coverage to persons receiving federally supported public assistance, it is a primary source of access to health care for families on AFDC. In addition to categorical entitlement, thirty-five states and the District of

Columbia also extend Medicaid eligibility to 'medically needy' individuals who do not qualify for public assistance but whose incomes are sufficiently low. In 1988, 23.9 million people qualified for Medicaid benefits at an expenditure of $48.7 billion. Adults and their children related to AFDC comprised the majority of beneficiaries (65%), but received a much smaller portion of Medicaid expenditures (24%).[9] Per capita payment was $583 to dependent children under the age of 21 and $1,069 to adults in families with dependent children (Green Book, 1990, pp. 1192-1198).

In addition, public transfers to families with children are also provided through tax benefits under the earned income tax credit and the dependent care tax credit. As of 1988, these tax credits provided about $8.3 billion in assistance to these families (Green Book, 1989, p.792 & p.798).

How much do these transfers benefit poor children in the United States? No state provides AFDC benefit levels sufficient to take a family above the poverty threshold. Levitan (1990) suggests that "the real value of the median state's maximum monthly AFDC payment declined by 37% between 1970 and 1989, to $360 for a family of three--only 46% of the official poverty threshold" (p. 49). Levitan (1990) further indicates that nine states (all in the South) pay a maximum benefit of less than a third of the poverty threshold: Alabama and Mississippi pay at most 15% of the poverty standard. However, the availability of food stamps brings this distressing picture to a somewhat better level, because AFDC families are eligible for food stamps, and more than four-fifths receive them (Levitan, 1990, p.49). The level of AFDC maximum benefit combined with food stamps in the median state in 1988 was $570 for a family of three. However, this combined level of benefits is still not sufficient to combat poverty, accounting for only 73% of the poverty line (Levitan, 1990, p.49).

To investigate the antipoverty impacts of transfers, Danziger (1989a) presented the percentage of pretransfer poor persons who were removed from poverty through the receipt of transfers. Danziger found that in 1985 welfare and nonwelfare transfers provided some financial aid to more than three-quarters of all pretransfer poor children. However, only 17% of all pretransfer poor children were taken out of poverty due to these transfers, which included cash benefits, food stamps, and energy assistance. More than 60% of pretransfer poor children received certain benefits but remained in poverty, and 23% received nothing. This antipoverty effect of 17% for children contrasts with the 77% for the elderly. Moreover, the author indicates that the antipoverty effect of transfers for children was smaller in 1985 than it was in 1975.

Danziger (1989a) further discusses the likelihood of escaping poverty by working more. First, the author considers parents who were pretransfer poor but received no transfer (23% of pretransfer poor). According to the author, this group worked substantial amounts (34 weeks or more) and earned about $159 per week on average, but fell through all safety nets. More surprisingly, their poverty gap was very large: $4263 for blacks; $4373 for hispanics; and $5390 for whites. Danziger (1989a) emphasizes that an additional 15 weeks of work per year among this group would cut the existing poverty gap by at most half. As a second group, the author considers parents who remained poor even after receiving transfers: this group worked somewhat fewer weeks (10 weeks for blacks and 17 weeks for whites) and tended to receive chiefly welfare benefits. Mean transfers for these families ranged from $4500 to $6000 depending on racial-ethnic group. The mean poverty gap for this group was still big: $4589 for blacks, $4226 for hispanics, and $3488 for whites. Because of the lack of labor force attachment, this group of parents was less likely to escape poverty on their own. All these results indicate that neither current transfer programs nor parents' work efforts is likely to significantly reduce the number of poor children.

A RESEARCH OBJECTIVE:
ISSUE OF INCOME-TESTING VERSUS
NON-INCOME-TESTING

I have discussed the poor circumstances in which children live in the United States, and briefly presented current federal programs for enhancing children's economic well-being. Although these programs alleviate poverty problems to some degree, we still observe that child poverty continues. Arguably, as addressed by Corbett (1993), there are "serious deficiencies in the way the U.S. conducts public policy for the child population" (p.5).

As mentioned earlier, most public transfer programs for children are characterized by income-testing.[10] The AFDC program, as the most important source of transfers for children, is strongly income tested, in that the defined family's income must be below a certain standard level established by the state of residence and that its benefits decline as earnings or other income sources increase. The food stamp program is income-tested as well, because of asset and income counts for eligibility and benefit levels. Medicaid, as a major public transfer of medical care for children, is also based on income-testing. Indeed, most welfare reforms in the United States have been long-standing but futile efforts to correct the adverse effects deeply rooted in this income-testing nature. We should admit that all welfare reforms during the past decades have actually failed to improve the economic well-being of children. This failure raises the fundamental question of whether the current system--consisting mainly of income-tested transfers--proceeds in the right direction. As addressed by one scholar, "the closer we move to pure welfare programs, the more difficult the value dilemmas become" (Ellwood, 1988, p.43). It may be time to search for a different direction. In this search, we face the important policy question of what the costs and benefits are of the alternative of non-income-tested transfers. This study is intended to assess the relative economic performance of this alternative approach--non-income-tested transfers.

The debate over the merits of income-tested versus non-income-tested transfer has a long history. In the United States, according to Garfinkel (1982), it goes back to the 1820s when the issue arose in connection with the provision for free public education.[11] However, the more fundamental issue of income-testing was raised in launching the 'War on Poverty' in the 1960s. As an explicit goal of public policy was designated as poverty elimination, the issue of debate became whether a children's allowance or a negative income tax (NIT) would provide a better aid to the working poor (Garfinkel, 1982). The idea of a negative income tax was that "just as the Internal Revenue Service collected taxes based on income and family size, it could pay out benefits (called negative taxes) based on income and family size to people with low income" (Garfinkel and McLanahan, 1986, p.111). Although there were some differences in the NIT proposal and the welfare program, they shared the common feature of being based on income-testing. On the other hand, benefit payments under a children's allowance would be made independently of income level but on the basis of the number of children in the family. The policy choice of these different approaches (that is, income-tested transfer or non-income-tested transfer) raised a fundamental question: which one is more efficient and more effective?

In earlier debates on the income-testing issue, advocates of non-income-tested programs argued that "income-tested programs stigmatize the poor, reduce social cohesion, and provide less aid to the poor" (Garfinkel, 1982, p.14). On the other hand, advocates of income-tested programs argued that "income-tested programs could be administered to treat beneficiaries with dignity, that the alleged social cohesion costs of income-tested programs were small or nonexistent, that non-income-tested programs would be costly, and that non-income-tested programs would provide less aid to the poor within budget constraints" (Garfinkel, 1982, p.14).

The most controversial debate over alternative transfer schemes has been the efficiency issue. A major rationale for the conventional approach--income-tested transfer--stems from a criterion of target efficiency. Target efficiency is defined as "the proportion of total transfer benefits accruing to some poor target groups--usually the pretransfer groups" (Kesselman and Garfinkel, 1978, p.183). From the viewpoint of target efficiency, non-income-tested benefits are a very inefficient means for helping those with low income, since the benefits are not concentrated where the need is greatest. However, the measure of target efficiency alone has a critical shortcoming: it ignores the effects of tax rates on work efforts. According to Kesselman and Garfinkel (1978), the essential difference between an income-tested program and a non-income-tested program is in the structure of their marginal tax rates. These authors define income-tested transfer as "one in which marginal tax rates on the poor exceed those on the nonpoor" (Kesselman and Garfinkel, 1978, p.185). Higher tax rates on the poor are a consequence of limiting transfer payments to the poor. In order to confine benefits to the poor, income-tested programs reduce benefits as income rises. By contrast, according to Kesselman and Garfinkel (1978), marginal tax rates under a non-income-tested transfer may be either constant or increase as income increases. This fundamental difference between the two transfer regimes--the marginal tax rate--is the key for measuring the economic efficiency of alternative approaches. On the grounds of economic efficiency, Kesselman and Garfinkel further argue that a non-income-tested transfer may be more efficient than an income-tested one.

However, the empirical findings are inconclusive. Some research on the relative ranking of alternative approaches has been conducted,[12] but the findings have been inconsistent and even contradicting. Moreover, most previous studies have compared economic performances based on a single program (for example, a negative income tax compared to a children's allowance). No previous study has investigated the effects of combined non-income-tested programs.

To investigate this issue, three policy changes--all providing non-income-tested benefits--are proposed for income transfers for families with children: (a) replacing the current child support system with a child support assurance system (CSAS); (b) replacing income tax deductions for children with a children's allowance; (c) replacing Medicaid and employer-provided insurance with national health insurance (NHI). By introducing these combined non-income-tested programs, I assume that there will be a shift in the transfer regime for families with children from an 'income-tested' to a 'non-income-tested' regime. Although these proposals include no exact substitution of a non-income-tested program for the income-tested program,[13] this shift can occur on two grounds. First, the proportion of non-income-tested programs in the total expenditure would increase, simply because of increased outlays for non-income-tested benefits. Second, the three non-income-tested programs would enable current AFDC recipients to exit welfare programs, and thus the relative size of welfare caseloads and expenditures would further shrink. In terms of the relative size of program caseloads and expenditures, therefore, it is expected that the weight of the transfer system as a whole would shift from 'income-tested' to 'non-income-tested.' As the non-income-tested programs prevail and dominate, current welfare programs eventually would become transitory assistance programs.

To estimate the costs and benefits of the new non-income-tested regime, the following research questions are to be answered:

(1) What would be the poverty incidence and gap under the three combined programs of the non-income-tested regime, compared to those under the current income-tested regime?

(2) How much would non-income-tested programs decrease AFDC caseloads and save AFDC benefits? As a result, how much

would off-AFDC cases subsequently decrease Medicaid recipiency and its expenditures?

(3) What impact would the non-income-tested regime have on food stamp participation and its benefit expenditures?

(4) What effects would the three non-income-tested programs have on income redistribution?

(5) What impact would they have on the labor supply?

(6) What would be the total cost? When financing schedules and savings are taken into account, what would be the net cost to the public?

(7) Is there any potential interaction effect which results from the combined programs?

The final question concerns an incremental effect that may result when three non-income-tested programs are combined. In other words, are the benefits and costs of a package of universal programs equivalent to the additive effects of each program performed by itself? Is the whole greater than the sum of the parts? Depending on the direction and the size of interaction of the combined programs, the estimated effects could be linearly additive or magnified as additional non-income-tested programs are added. The final objective of this study is to examine the degree to which the estimated effects would be altered when several non-income-tested programs are combined, and identify the direction and magnitude of that interaction.

A variety of issues are involved with income-testing and non-income-testing (i.e., their effects on family break-ups, stigma, social cohesion, and fostering bureaucracy). This research cannot provide a comprehensive assessment covering all these questions. This evaluation of non-income-tested reform, thus, is limited in the sense that my assessment is made with a focus on its economic performance and ignoring its non-economic effects. In addition, this study ignores the administrative side of income-tested versus non-income-tested programs.

To analyze the research questions listed above, this study employs a microsimulation method in a static context. The use of the microsimulation approach was originally encouraged by the movements of the War on Poverty in the 1960s and 1970s. The initiation of many of the War on Poverty programs created an enormous need for reliable estimates of program costs and effects. To obtain systematic information, the Reforms in Income Maintenance (RIM) was first designed and programmed for President Johnson's Commission on income maintenance programs in 1969 (Wilensky, 1970). The RIM was developed to evaluate a number of alternative negative income tax and other welfare reform plans. In 1970, the RIM model was further extended and modified to test various versions of the Family Assistance Plan (FAP) proposed by President Nixon (Webb, Michel, & Bergsman, 1989).[14] Since then, a variety of microsimulation models have been developed and extensively used to assess particular policy proposals.[15]

Typically, any policy change or proposal raises a number of important questions that should be answered: What are the net costs as well as total outlays required by a particular plan? What is the size of efficiency loss associated with the plan? What is the number of potential recipients? What is the benefit distribution among different demographic and economic groups? What is the change in income distribution? What program parameters would minimize certain adverse effects at reasonable costs? The microsimulation method has been a policy-analysis tool for answering these questions based on income and demographic information at the household level. In other words, microsimulation is a model for constructing the current tax and income transfer system and introducing the specific changes of policy proposal at the household level in order to estimate the costs and impacts of the proposal.

In particular, the microsimulation method provides the following advantages for my research purpose. First, microsimulation can incorporate behavior responses to proposed policy changes. Any policy change in the transfer system implies changes in income guarantee and implicit tax rate which further affect an individual's behavioral decisions such as program participation and labor supply. The ability of microsimulation to incorporate behavioral responses is important, particularly because it provides a more reliable estimate of net program cost. For example, in the absence of any behavioral change due to the proposal, the program net cost would be equal to benefit outlays. However, if the proposal has any incentive or disincentive effect, the net cost which takes account of behavioral responses would be different from simple benefit outlays. To the extent that program costs depend on the responses of individuals, a more reliable cost estimate can be obtained through incorporating their empirical relationships. In addition, this study takes into account financing schedules, and microsimulation also can model behavioral responses to increased tax rates for financing.

Second, microsimulation can capture distributional features of narrowly defined sectors--by demographic group, by income class, or by government and private sector. The ability of microsimulation to produce distributional information is important, particularly for such policy questions as who is gaining and who is losing (Haveman, 1987). This ability stems from the fact that microsimulation is performed on microdata rather than the aggregated data base. Using detailed information on the individual characteristics of a population, microsimulation can figure out who would be eligible for a new program or program change, who would gain and who would lose if the change were implemented. From simulated microunit outputs, microsimulation can generate univariate and multivariate distributions, and aggregate these microunit outputs for the relevant subgroups in question.

Third, microsimulation can model the linkages and interdependence of different programs or different sectors of the economy. We know that public transfers themselves have complicated linkages among them. In constructing and programming the simulation model, public transfer is considered as a "interacting" system consisting of several components. Furthermore, the public transfer system can be considered as having interdependence with other economic systems, and that interdependence of economic systems can be modelled.[16] In particular, the ability of the microsimulation method to model the interdependence of different programs is important for my study purpose, not only because it allows the benefit package of several welfare programs to be taken into account in program participation and work decisions, but also because it allows the interaction of current programs and post-reform programs.

Finally, the design of policy programs always involves conflicting objectives, and thus trade-offs need to be negotiated so as to achieve a program structure that maximizes some desired goals at least cost. Microsimulation allows a wide range of policy alternatives to be analyzed and assessed, so that the optimal program parameters can be selected. Especially by incorporating behavior responses and generating distributional information, microsimulation can provide the trade-off between equity and efficiency associated with alternative program parameters.[17]

Notes

1. See Smolensky, Danziger, and Gottschalk (1988); Smeeding, Torrey, and Rein (1988).

2. Most poverty statistics are taken from Bureau of the Census (1992).

3. Some other factors affecting child poverty in the United States, found in the existing literature, include an increased inequality in the distribution of income; a sluggish macroeconomic environment that lowered the real incomes of families in all economic strata; and stagnant wages for young workers.

4. See Bane and Ellwood (1986); Duncan, Coe, and Hill (1984); Duncan and Hoffman (1985).

5. The percent of children with employer-related insurance declined from 66% in 1980 to 63% in 1990. See Monheit and Cunningham (1992), p. 156; also see Sheils and Wolfe (1992), p.116.

6. In addition to the food stamp program, federal food assistance focusing on child nutrition provides a variety of supplemental programs supplying breakfast, lunch, and milk to more than 30 million children in private and public schools and day care centers, at a federal cost of $4.5 billion in 1989. Also, the special food assistance program for women, infants, and children (WIC) and the commodity supplemental food program -- which channels aid to low-income, pregnant, and postpartum women and to infants and children up to age five whose inadequate diets may endanger their health -- provide for almost 4 million persons at a cost of $2.0 billion. See Levitan (1990), p.105.

7. Those deductions in 1988 include the standard deduction ($106), 20% of earned income, out-of-pocket dependent care expenses (up to $160), and shelter expenses (exceeding half of income after other deductions and ceiling at $170).

8. In addition to Medicaid, some other federal programs have sought to improve access to health care for the poor. These include community health centers in low-income areas and federal block grant funds for

maternal and child health. In 1989, the federal government spent $415 million to support 550 primary community health center facilities, serving five million patients. A federal block grant of $554 million in 1989 was allocated to states for maternal and child health (Levitan, 1990, p.87).

9. On the other hand, the elderly and the disabled receive almost three quarters of Medicaid expenditures. A large portion of Medicaid is spent to pay for nursing home care of the elderly receiving supplemental security income which is not available under Medicare.

10. Another pronounced characteristic of U.S. transfers for children is categorical. AFDC is categorical in the sense that benefits are more confined to mother-only families; food stamps and Medicaid are categorical as well because of entitlement being closely linked to welfare groups such as those receiving AFDC and SSI.

11. The author also indicates that many had favored subsidizing the education of only the poor, but by about 1850 the issue had been settled in favor of universal free public education. See Garfinkel (ed.) (1982), pp. 5-6.

12. See Barth (1972); Betson et al. (1982); Garfinkel and Haveman (1974); Musgrave et. al (1970); Kesselman and Garfinkel (1978); Rea (1974); Sadka et. al (1982).

13. An alternative study could propose to substitute, for example, children's allowance for the AFDC program, and estimate its costs and effects. This would be another way of investigating the income-testing versus non-income-testing issue.

14. The RIM model became the antecedent of TRIM and TRIM2. See Webb et al. (1989) for more details.

15. See Lewis and Michel (1989) for the detailed characteristics of these simulation models.

16. Although microsimulation can model policy-induced changes in other economic systems (e.g., price and industry systems) on the second-, third- and fourth-round, this study ignores these macro effects.

17.On the other hand, the use of microsimulation entails some disadvantages. These disadvantages will be discussed in the section on study limitations in chapter 6.

II

U.S. Policy Initiatives and
A Proposed New Regime

This chapter consists of two sections. The first section will describe the nation's strategies to combat child poverty, and reform approaches for dealing with the problems of the existing transfer system during the past two decades. This section presents the historical trend in policy initiatives for families with children. The second section offers a conceptual understanding of the proposed non-income-tested programs-- child support assurance system, children's allowance, and national health insurance. For each of these programs, the section also includes an overview of existing proposals.

U.S. POLICY INITIATIVES FOR CHILDREN DURING THE PAST DECADES

Income transfer policy for families with children has been a questionable issue, in part because of the increase in transfers during the past decades and the large proportion of the federal budget they constitute. It is also questionable because it involves a choice over the fundamentally conflicting values of efficiency and equity. Although economists articulate the trade-off between efficiency and equity,[1] policy makers often face the difficulty of striking a balance between them. Over the past two decades, we have seen four strands of emphasis in policy initiatives for both improving the economic status of children and attaining the self-sufficiency of their caretakers. These strands are welfare reform, private child support enforcement, health care reform, and tax reform.

Welfare Reform

The term of welfare in the United States has typically been identified with the AFDC program. Because AFDC is the most visible in-cash program for poor children, welfare reform has often been considered as "a significant modification of the scope, generosity, design, or administration of that program" (Corbett, 1993, p.1).

The AFDC program (originally ADC or Aid to Dependent Children) was incorporated virtually without debate into the Social Security Act of 1935 (Berkowitz, 1991). The program was designed to support impoverished widows so that they could fully devote themselves to their caretaker responsibilities for children. It was expected that the program would diminish as Social Security matured to absorb more and more widows and children under Survivors' insurance (Garfinkel and McLanahan, 1986). By the 1960s, however, it became apparent that AFDC had not been shrunk as expected. Because the program was expanding rather than declining, it became a major target of criticism for eroding work efforts and resulting in a 'welfare trap', causing marital break-ups, being an ineffective benefit system, being administratively costly, and stigmatizing recipients. In particular, most public concern was directed at its work disincentive effect. Before 1962,[2] AFDC payments in most states were reduced by one dollar for each dollar earned by recipients (Garfinkel and McLanahan, 1986, p.107). Taking into account the expenses incurred in working (e.g., transportation and child care costs), many AFDC recipients were worse off financially if they chose to work. Thus, most welfare reforms were intended to minimize or eliminate this adverse effect, although their approaches were somewhat different.

Under the federal government's lead, several national plans were considered in the 1960s, ranging from universal demogrants to variants of the negative income tax concept. The negative income tax (NIT) particularly appealed to economists by the mid-1960s. The basic idea of NIT was to modify a central feature of the welfare benefit--the high marginal tax rate implied in AFDC benefit reduction as income rose. Advocates of negative income tax believed that work disincentives would be minimized by lowering the benefit reduction rate (a 50% benefit reduction rate is a frequent one in proposed NIT plans). The NIT idea was first incorporated into practical policy in 1967, when Congress amended the AFDC program to permit beneficiaries to keep the first thirty dollars earned each month plus one of every three dollars earned in excess of thirty dollars. When President Nixon took office in 1969, a variant of NIT called as the Family Assistance Plan was officially proposed but failed to be enacted (Garfinkel and McLanahan, 1986, pp.111-115).

Continuing concern about work incentives shifted toward enforcing work requirements in the 1970s. The 1972 amendment to the AFDC program required AFDC mothers with no children under age 6 to register for work. Although this work requirement was never effectively enforced, by the mid-1970s the attitude that welfare mothers should work became prevailing. Accordingly, a variety of work provisions subsequently evolved, including large-scale demonstration and experimental work programs (Garfinkel and McLanahan, 1986, p. 115-116).[3]

However, all these strategies virtually failed to take many AFDC families out of welfare dependency or to enhance their economic situation. Welfare rolls continued to rise. The idea of negative income tax to provide work incentives was officially abandoned in 1981, when the Reagan administration repealed the earnings disregard rule for those working more than four months (Wong, 1988). By the early 1980s, the nation witnessed a new paradigm clearly emerging. As expressed by one scholar, "explanations of poverty shifted more toward individual factors (i.e., behavioral failure) and away from institutional factors (i.e., market failure); the 'underclass' issue gained scholarly attention; and the locus of action shifted to the states" (Corbett, 1993, p.3). Accordingly, the strategy of solution shifted from work incentives toward mandatory work requirements in return for benefits. This shift consequently made welfare even more restrictive. This renewed attention to so called 'workfare' was embodied in the Omnibus Budget Reconciliation Act (OBRA) of 1981,[4] which allowed the states to replace cash relief with work relief.[5] Under workfare, AFDC recipients work in exchange for their relief checks. The mid-1980s have been characterized by state experimentation with incremental welfare reform programs providing training and employment services to long-term, nonworking welfare recipients.[6] Based on these experiences, Congress passed the Family Support Act in 1988. This bill embodied the "new consensus" of redirecting welfare policy, particularly for the nonworking poor. It extended the AFDC program for unemployed two-parent families, but added a requirement that at least one of the parents engage in community service in return for benefits.

Welfare reform has been a long standing concern and issue among politicians, policy-makers, and academics. Although a variety of welfare reforms have been proposed and tested, AFDC has remained the same program in its central feature that was formed sixty years ago in the Social Security Act. It is still a categorical program, because benefits are restricted to a certain demographic group (i.e., single mothers with children). It is also a welfare program in that benefits decrease or cease altogether as income level increases. We have seen that welfare reform is futile because of the dilemma of the so-called 'iron triangle': welfare is an attempt to achieve three mutually conflicting goals at the same time--reducing poverty at a given budget constraint without eroding incentives to work.

Enforcing Private Child Support

The tremendous increase in the prevalence of single-mother families and the growth in public expenditures on them provoked political attention in the mid-1970s to the role of absent parents.[7] The national emphasis on private child support collection was initiated by creating Title IV-D of the Social Security Amendment in 1975. Under this legislation, a federal Office of Child Support Enforcement (OCSE) was established and the Office, along with its state counterparts, took the responsibility for collecting child support in all AFDC cases, and in non-AFDC cases if requested. The legislation also established a national network of federal and state parent locator services (Garfinkel and McLanahan, 1986).

By the early 1980s, the federal government's interest in enforcement of private child support obligations as a method of reducing welfare expenditures had grown. The 1984 Child Support Enforcement Amendments went beyond the objective of reducing AFDC costs and caseloads (Garfinkel and McLanahan, 1986, p.136). Under this legislation, child support enforcement was applied not only to parents whose children were on AFDC, but also to all parents whose children were potentially eligible for child support. The Amendments included two most important provisions: all states were required to establish statewide guidelines for award levels; states were also required to adopt automatic income withholding if the noncustodial payments were delinquent for one month. In addition, the 1984 legislation changed the treatment of child support payments in the AFDC program. Previously, each dollar received in child support had reduced the AFDC benefit by one dollar (Garfinkel and McLanahan, 1986, p.137). To create incentives for custodial mothers on AFDC to secure awards, the first $50 of child support payment was to be disregarded in calculating AFDC benefits. As part of the Amendments, Congress further authorized the state of Wisconsin to demonstrate a new child support assurance program.

The 1988 Family Support Act immensely strengthened the 1984 guidelines and income-withholding provisions. While the 1984 Amendments allowed the courts to ignore the guidelines, the 1988 legislation made the guidelines the presumptive child support award, which meant that departures from the guidelines had to be justified in writing and subject to review by a higher court (Garfinkel, 1992, p.29 & p.31). Furthermore, the 1988 Act required states, by 1993, to review child support awards of Title IV-D cases (those being handled by the Office of Child Support Enforcement) at least every three years (Garfinkel, 1992, p.29). With respect to routine income withholding, the 1988 legislation required withholding of the child support obligation from the outset for all Title IV-D cases as of 1990, and for all child support cases as of 1994 (Garfinkel, 1992, p.31). This contrasted with the previous legislation (1984) which had required withholding only in cases of delinquency.

Indeed, enforcement of child support reflects a social agreement that government intervention in collection of private money is necessary to ensure children's well being. The strategy also reflects a strong statement on the absent parents' responsibility for their children. This is another notable trend in the U.S. history of transfer policy for children over the past two decades.

Health Care Reform

During the 1960s, as the federal government was expanding its role for social policy, Medicaid was created (in 1965) as an additional component in the Social Security Act. Since then, Medicaid has become the most important public health care program for low-income households. Originally, Medicaid was designed as a categorical entitlement, specifically for mothers and children on the AFDC program, and for aged, blind, or disabled persons receiving Supplemental Security Income (SSI).[8] Medicaid was a joint program in which federal grants were provided to the states on a cost-sharing basis to pay for medical services for the poor. States, however, retained significant flexibility in establishing income eligibility criteria, defining limits on the coverage of services, and setting payment rates for providers.

During the first ten years after it was created, Medicaid had an expanding period in eligibility and expenditures, largely due to the rapid growth of AFDC caseloads. The second decade of the program, however, was a period of retrenchment, particularly for children's health services. Beginning in 1972, according to Sardell (1990), there was a shift within Medicaid away from spending on health services for children, as a higher proportion of Medicaid funds went to pay for services for aged, blind, and disabled SSI recipients (p.279). Sardell (1990) indicates that in 1972, 18% of total Medicaid expenditures paid for services for non-disabled children under age 21; by 1987, the proportion was down to 13% (p.279). Most retrenchment of Medicaid for children's health care was made in the early 1980s, as part of the Reagan administration's effort to reduce spending for social programs. The Omnibus Budget Reconciliation Act of 1981 (OBRA-1981) reduced the federal government's share of Medicaid for three years and restricted Medicaid eligibility for children of working parents by limiting the gross income of such families applying for AFDC (Oberg and Polich, 1988, p.87). In addition, the reduction in federal spending for Medicaid was accompanied by the creation of block grants to the states to replace categorical health services programs (Sardell, 1990, p.279). OBRA-1981 also eliminated other child health programs initiated in the 1960s.[9]

By 1984, however, there was renewed national attention to children's health. Beginning in 1984, Congress enacted a series of reforms which broadened the number of children and pregnant women eligible for the Medicaid program and which separated Medicaid from the AFDC program, to which it had long been linked (Sardell, 1990, p.280). Under the Deficit Reduction Act of 1984, the states were required to provide Medicaid for all pregnant women and for children under age 5 in families whose income and resources were within AFDC standards but who did not meet other AFDC criteria (such as having two parents present). The subsequent set of Medicaid reforms were provisions of the 1986 and 1987 Omnibus Reconciliation Acts.

OBRA-1986 permitted states to ignore asset tests in determining Medicaid eligibility for pregnant women and for children under age 5, and to grant automatic eligibility to pregnant women while their applications were being processed and for sixty days after they gave birth (Sardell, 1990, p.281). Under OBRA-1986, states were also allowed to phase in Medicaid coverage for children under age 8 in families with incomes between the AFDC eligibility standard and the poverty threshold. OBRA-1987 allowed states to include all pregnant women and infants with family incomes up to 185% of the poverty level (Sardell, 1990, p.281). In 1988, as part of the Medicare Catastrophic Coverage Act, Congress further mandated that states phase in coverage for children 6 to 19 years old in families with incomes up to 100% of the poverty level so that all children in this category would be covered by 2002 (Green Book, 1990, p.1406).

As a result of this series of federally mandated Medicaid expansions, states are now required to cover all pregnant women and children 0 to 6 years old in families with incomes up to 133% of the official poverty level (Green Book, 1990, p.1406). In addition, states may expand coverage for this group to include those with incomes up to 185% of the poverty level.

In spite of these reforms to expand Medicaid coverage, certain limitations remain. As Lewit et al. (1992) indicate, the most pervasive obstacles to health care access for both pregnant women and children on Medicaid are inadequate provider participation in Medicaid and an inadequate supply of providers in neighborhoods where poor families live (p. 16). The authors also indicate that low reimbursement rates and administrative complexities which make obtaining reimbursement costly and problematic have resulted in low and declining rates of participation in Medicaid programs by obstetrical care providers and pediatricians (Lewit et al., 1992, p.16). Moreover, the Medicaid program leaves out many poor children without other medical coverage. As mentioned in chapter 1, the program covers only one-third of the children in poverty. In addition, the lack of private coverage for children emphasizes that health reform efforts should go beyond the welfare type of Medicaid which is limited only to the poor. Recent attention to a universal health care system reflects nationwide dissatisfactions with the current health-care system.

Tax Reform

In addition to those major emphases in the nation's policy initiatives for children (including welfare reform, enforcement of private child support, and health care reform), the U.S. also has sought for reformative efforts in the income tax system. The most prominent provision of the tax system for assisting families with children is the earned income tax credit (EITC). EITC was originally enacted in 1975 as a way to relieve the burden of the social security payroll tax on low-wage working parents with children (Scholz, 1993, pp.1-2). The original EITC equaled 10% of the first $4000 of earned income (i.e., a maximum credit of $400), and was phased out at a rate of 10 cents per dollar of earnings (or adjusted gross income, whichever was higher) for incomes between $4000 and $8000 (Green Book, 1991, p.897).

Since then, several pieces of legislation have adjusted the maximum credit and income ranges for eligibility. For 1979 through 1984, the maximum credit was increased to $500 (10% of the first $5000 of earned income). Also, the income level at which the phaseout began was raised to $6000, with a complete phaseout not occurring until an income level of $10,000. For 1985 and 1986, the maximum credit was increased to $550 (11% of the first $5000 of earned income), and the credit was phased out beginning at $6000 of income and ending at $11,000. Under the Tax Reform Act of 1986 (beginning in 1987), the dollar amount of EITC began to be indexed for inflation; the basic credit rate was increased to 14%; the phaseout range of incomes was set between $6920 and $15432 (1987 dollars) (Green Book, 1991, p.897).

The most significant change was made in the Omnibus Budget Reconciliation Act of 1990 (OBRA 1990). OBRA 1990 substantially increased the maximum amount of the basic credit and added an adjustment to reflect family size. For 1991, the basic EITC rate was 16.7% for taxpayers with one qualifying child (maximum credit of $1192) and 17.3% for those with two or more children (maximum credit of $1235). EITC was phased out for taxpayers with adjusted gross income (AGI) (or, if greater, earned income) above $11,250 at a rate of 11.93 cents[10] for each dollar of AGI over the threshold. The basic EITC was completely phased out for AGI above $21,242 in 1991. (Green Book, 1991, p.897). Another legislation in 1993 has brought even bigger changes in EITC. Phasing in through 1996, the basic EITC rate will increase to 34% for low-wage earners with one child, and 40% for those with two or more children.

Another tax provision that benefits families with children is the dependent care credit. Under the section 21 of the Internal Revenue Code, a tax credit is allowed with respect to certain employment-related expenses for dependent care. The origin of the credit was a provision enacted in 1954, providing a deduction to employed women, widowers, and legally separated or divorced men for certain employment-related dependent care expenses. Generally, a qualifying individual was a child under the age of 15, or a physically or mentally incapacitated dependent or spouse (Green Book, 1991, pp.906-907).

The Tax Reduction Act of 1976 replaced the deduction with a non-refundable credit, which made the dependent credit more attractive. From 1976 to 1988, utilization of the dependent care credit increased from 2.7 to 9.0 million families (Green Book, 1991, p.908). However, changes made in the Family Support Act of 1988 reduced the attractiveness of the program. In particular, the 1988 Act provided that a child must be under the age of 13 (rather than 15) to be treated as a qualifying individual (Green Book, 1991, p.906).

In 1991, a non-refundable credit against income tax liability was available for up to 30% of a limited amount of dependent care expenses. Eligible employment-related dependent care expenses were limited to $2400 (if one qualifying individual), or $4800 (if two or more) (Green Book, 1991, p.907).

A NEW REGIME:
PROPOSED NON-INCOME-TESTED PROGRAMS

In the previous section, I discussed U.S. reform approaches during the past decades. Despite a variety of reform strategies having been tried, we are still observing problems and struggling to search for better solutions. For a new regime of improving children's economic well-being, I propose three non-income-tested transfer programs: child support assurance system, children's allowance, and national health insurance. By non-income-tested regime, I mean that these three programs are to be implemented all together. This section will present the characteristics and background of each element program and describe existing proposals for it.

Child Support Assurance System (CSAS)

A large part of the poverty problem, as mentioned in the previous chapter, is associated with single parenthood. A natural response to this phenomenon has been directed to a national emphasis on parental responsibility for supporting children, particularly by a noncustodial parent. To understand the nature of relatively low child support payments under the current system, three dimensions can be considered: first, a child support order may not be established (i.e., award establishment); second, the amount of the obligation may be too low (award level); finally, even after a custodial parent obtains an award at a decent level, the child support may not be paid (child support collection). Poor child support payments reflect the failure at all of these stages of the current private child support system (Garfinkel, 1992).

As an alternative to the inadequate current system of private child support, Garfinkel and Melli (1982), in the early 1980s, proposed the child support assurance system (CSAS). The philosophical premise underlying the CSAS is that both custodial and noncustodial parents are responsible for sharing income with their children and the government is responsible for assuring that children who live apart from their parents receive the share to which they are entitled (Garfinkel, 1992, p.45). Specifically, the CSAS has three major components (Garfinkel and Melli, 1982): (a) a uniform percentage standard for establishing child support obligations; (b) immediate withholding of the child support obligation from wages and other sources of income of the noncustodial parent; and (c) an assured or minimum-guaranteed child support benefit for each family.[11]

The first component addresses the need for a standard of award level for child support. For the standard level of award, the CSAS adopts a simple numerical formula in which child support obligation depends on the gross income of the noncustodial parent and the number of children to be supported. The formula for the standard is that for one child, the award be 17% of the noncustodial parent's gross income; for two children, 25%; and then 29%, 31%, and 34%

for three, four, and five or more children, respectively. Since the award is set as a percentage of income rather than as a flat dollar amount, it changes automatically with changes in noncustodial income (Garfinkel and Melli, 1982).

Second, the routine income withholding component is intended to increase child support collections once an award is determined. The idea is that the child support obligation is withheld from paychecks or other sources of noncustodial income in all child support cases, just like collecting income taxes and payroll taxes. The withheld money goes to the local Office of Child Support and is, in turn, sent to the custodial parent each month (Garfinkel and Melli, 1982).

The third, and perhaps most controversial, element of CSAS is the assured benefit, controversial because of the cost to the government. Although the CSAS assumes parental responsibility for children, some noncustodial parents may not earn enough to pay their child support obligations. An assured benefit will insure children against the risk that their absent parent will fail to pay child support (Garfinkel, 1992, p.47). When the noncustodial parent pays less than the assured level, the difference is made up by the government. This public benefit is universal, not income-tested, provided to all income classes. Because the assured benefit is non-income-tested, it is possible that custodial parents in the middle or upper classes will receive the assured benefit when their children's absent parents fail to pay. As a take-back of public money paid out to rich custodial parents, the public portion of the assured benefit (paid by the government) is counted as taxable income for the resident parent under the CSAS. Also, there are a couple of limits to eligibility, even though assured benefits are not income-tested. Assured benefits are limited only to those with awards, which is to induce custodial parents to secure child support awards. In addition, AFDC custodial parents are required to choose either CSAS or AFDC participation (Garfinkel and Melli, 1982).[12]

Since Garfinkel and Melli proposed the CSAS, a part of its elements has been embodied into child support legislation. The Family Support Act of 1988 requires states to make a child support standard presumptive, although it does not require that the state adopt a percentage standard. In addition, the 1988 Act requires immediate income withholding of the child support obligation to begin in 1990 for all new or modified orders being enforced by the Office of Child Support Enforcement, and for all child support cases as of 1994 (Green Book, 1990, p.679). As a result, by 1994 the automatic withholding provision of CSAS will be virtually implemented in all new child support cases in the United States. However, the assured benefit has not been implemented, although New York is currently field-testing a similar assured benefit program (Meyer et al., 1991a, p.8).

Children's Allowance

Children's allowance has drawn relatively little attention in the United States. Although some proposals for a children's allowance were made for a short time during the late 1960s and early 1970s, the United States has been the only major Western nation not having such a program (Brazer, 1968, p.141). As a means of income support for children, however, children's allowances have been adopted in some form by more than 62 nations, including all 27 European countries.[13]

According to Vadakin (1968), a children's allowance (or sometimes called 'family allowance') is defined as "systematic payments made to families with dependent children, either by employers or by the government, for the primary purpose of promoting the well-being of such children" (pp.2-3). This provides a broad definition in the sense that it includes the employment-related type of allowance for which eligibility is dependent on the existence of an employment relationship, and thus for which unemployed persons or those working in an uncovered industry are ineligible. A more narrow definition is given by Schorr (1966), who defined it as "regular payments for children made without regard to family income or other eligibility conditions" (p.147). By this definition, a children's allowance means a universal system covering all families with children that reside in the country. Thus, it does not include public assistance, survivors' insurance, or employment-related benefits for children.[14]

In addition to definition, the operation of the program allows for a variety of forms. First, coverage may begin with the first child (as in most countries), or start with the second child (as in Britain, for example). Similarly, allowances may commence with the third child (as in South Africa), or with the fourth child (as in Russia). In contrast, some countries favor children born earlier in order. Tunisia, for example, limits the coverage to the first four children in a family (Vadakin, 1968). Second, some variations can be found with respect to allowance payments: some countries provide a uniform rate of payments to all children, while other countries pay differential allowances based on the age or the birth order of the child. For example, in the former Canadian program, benefits were higher for older than for younger children. The British program, on the other hand, is based on the birth order of the child, with a progressive scale in which the third child (and subsequent children) receives a higher level of allowance than the second child does (Vadakin, 1968). Third, various methods of financing and administering the program may be employed. Where a universal program exists, benefits are usually financed from general tax revenues and are unrelated to social security, as in Canada and Britain. In some countries, such as France and Germany, the program is tied to social insurance and financed through payroll taxes imposed on employers (Vadakin, 1968). Finally, benefits may be counted as taxable income or excluded from taxable income (Vadakin, 1968).

In spite of the different forms of children's allowance, certain positions underlie any such program. The program constitutes a means of redistributing income in such a way as to benefit the child-rearing portion of a nation's population. Because it is intended to share the burden of child rearing, all families with dependent children are eligible to receive such grants as a matter of right, without resort to a means test, and regardless of income levels. Although some countries adopt a limited eligibility through employment status, the children's allowance is typically considered as a universal benefit available to all children residing in the country.[15] The children's allowance also can be seen as a method of adjusting, at least in some measure, the imbalance between family income and family need. As a family grows in size through the addition of children, its needs increase; unless the income of the family increases commensurately, the economic and social conditions of its members will be impaired. The children's allowance, in a sense, serves to supplement income particularly for a family of large size.

National Health Insurance (NHI)

American's health care system is often viewed as displeasing all parties, including health care providers, consumers, and payers. Although the United States ranks as the top in health care spending in the world, one out of every seven individuals lacks any health insurance coverage, and many more are inadequately covered (Lewin, 1993). During the past decades, concerns over a rapid increase in health care costs, inequitable coverage, and system inefficiencies have been expressed in various domestic agendas. More recently, major reform of the U.S. health care system has become a controversial issue across the country. More than 30 health care reform bills have been introduced in Congress, ranging from 'fine-tuning' the current system to substituting it for a universal health plan similar to that of Canada (Lewin, 1993). Various proposals can be classified into three broad categories: (a) single payer approach; (b) employer mandate approach including 'play or pay'; (c) tax credit approach. All proposals under each approach can not be described here. Instead, a few proposals will be selected to illustrate and characterize each of these approaches.

Single Payer Approach: The single payer approach is typically illustrated in Canada and the United Kingdom. Among various proposals for this approach in the United States, the proposal that would require the most restructuring of the health care system is found in Rep. Ronald Dellums's (D-Calif.) bill. This bill proposes to provide comprehensive services through a government-owned-and-operated health care system, to be financed by income, corporate, and payroll taxes (Brown, 1988). Moreover, the bill proposes that all health professionals and workers would be salaried.

   In contrast, the USHealth Act, proposed by Rep. Edward Roybal (D-Calif.), is a less controlled model in that health care providers would have freedom of choice for their practice. Roybal's bill proposes to integrate Medicare, Medicaid, and private insurance into a single public system, which would cover the entire population with comprehensive benefits including long-term care and preventive care. The bill also proposes that providers would be paid prospectively set fees based on Medicare payment schedules. To finance the program, Roybal's bill requires a coinsurance of from 20% to 25% up to a limit, a surcharge on existing corporate and individual tax liabilities for all tax payers, and eliminating both current income tax exemptions for employer contributions of premiums and the current wage cap on payroll taxes. However, people in poverty would be exempt from any cost sharing. As a cost containment, total national health spending is proposed to be capped at 12-13% of the GNP. Fees for health care providers would be indexed to this budget constraint (Roybal, 1991).

The proposal of the Physicians for a National Health Program (NHP)[16] is similar to Roybal's bill. It proposes to create a single insurer in each state that would replace Medicare, Medicaid, and private insurers, be locally controlled, but be subject to stringent national standards (Grumbach et al., 1991, P.2549). Everyone would be fully insured for all medically necessary services including prescription drugs and long-term care. Unlike Roybal's bill, all out-of-pocket payments such as copayments or deductibles would be eliminated. Like Roybal's proposal, the NHP would set the overall health care budget. To keep expenditures within target, each hospital would be given an annual global budget covering all operating expenses, and physicians would be given three options--fee-for-service; salaries from institutions receiving global budgets; or salaries from group practices or HMO's receiving capitation payments (Center for National Health Program Studies [CNHPS], 1992, P.104). The NHP would be financed by replacing current premiums with payroll taxes (with average tax rates of 9% for medium and large employers, 2% for employees, and half these rates for business with fewer than 20 employees); by adding a new income tax bracket of 38%; and by other increased or new federal tax sources (Grumbach, 1991, p.2552).

Although these proposals vary, some common features can be found. Under the single payer approach, the government is the single insurer for all basic health care services. This requires a substantial structural rearrangement of the current health care system. Thus, multiple private markets of health care would be undermined or replaced by a somewhat centralized system. Second, most proposals often adopt a concept of global budget or target expenditure to cap health care growth, which assumes that regulatory rather than voluntary efforts would bring about more effective cost containment. The single payer approach is often considered as a model that ensures equal access while controlling overall costs. Third, most proposals of this category retain 'freedom of choice,' in spite of centralized administration. Providers negotiate their fees within a global budget and people go to doctors and hospitals of their choice. Finally, most proposals based on a single payer system employ a government-financing method, even though the kind of tax employed may be different. This financing method is considered to have more potential for equity in distribution of health care burdens among different income classes. (Lewin, 1993, p.12).

Employer Mandate Approach: The employer mandate approach would expand current employer-based insurance so that all workers and their dependents would receive health coverage through their jobs. While this approach was first proposed by President Nixon in 1974 (CNHPS, 1992, p.119), many recent proposals have been called 'play or pay,' and include a strategy of managed care for cost containment. Among numerous proposals for this type of health reform, two structural variations can be considered. The first variation of employer mandate plan would require employers either to provide health insurance or to pay a tax on payroll to buy workers and their dependents into a public plan (play or pay mandate); the second variation of the plan would simply require employers to provide health insurance for all workers and their dependents (straight mandate) (Zedlewski et al., 1993).

The 'play or pay' mandate is illustrated in the 'HealthAmerica' bill[17] introduced by Sen. George Mitchell (D-ME). This bill requires all employers to either 'play' by purchasing private health insurance for employees working at least 17.5 hours per week and their dependents, or 'pay' into a public program by making a 7-8% contribution based on payroll (Silow-Carroll and Meyer, 1993, pp.211-212). All nonelderly who are not covered through employers would be required to participate in the public program. The public program is proposed to be administered by the states and replace the current Medicaid program (except for long-term care service) (Silow-Carroll and Meyer, 1993, p.212). Medicare, however, would continue to cover the elderly population. The Mitchell bill requires that employers who 'play' offer an approved minimum health benefit package, and that the public plan provide the benefit package identical to the basic employer-based plan. For cost sharing, employees and their dependents covered through employers would be required to pay 20% of the premium, a deductible set at $250 per person, and a coinsurance rate of 20% up to $3000 per year (Silow-Carroll and Meyer, 1993, p.211). Those enrolled in the public plan would be required to pay premiums tied to an individual's ability to pay.[18] The public program would be financed by federal, state, employer, and individual contributions. Providers would be reimbursed at the equivalent of current Medicare rates. To achieve cost control, the Mitchell bill emphasizes the use of global budgets and corresponding fee schedules.

On the other hand, the Bill Clinton proposal outlined during his presidential campaign[19] represents the 'straight' employer mandate.

The Clinton plan requires employers to provide coverage directly to workers or to purchase their coverage through 'purchasing groups.' The purchasing groups would pool small businesses and individuals so that they would be able to negotiate with competing private insurers and buy the 'best' plan offered (Silow-Carroll and Meyer, 1993, p.215). Unlike Mitchell's public program (state-administered), Clinton's purchasing groups would be privately operated, while publicly sponsored by government subsidies (Silow-Carroll and Meyer, 1993, p.216). For employees whose employers choose to join purchasing groups, the public subsidy would be the difference between the sum of employer and employee contributions and the cost of coverage.[20] For part-time workers who do not qualify for the new employer plan, and the unemployed who are ineligible for Medicaid, the subsidy would be the difference between their income-related contributions and the cost of coverage. The Clinton proposal also includes an increase in the health insurance tax exemption for the self-employed from the current 25% to 100% (Silow-Carroll and Meyer, 1993, p.216). Similar to the Mitchell plan, the Clinton proposal involves national and state budget goals of health care to control costs, but puts greater emphasis on 'managed competition' among health-care networks.

While various employer mandate proposals differ in their details, most share several common features.[21] First, the major difference from the single payer approach is that employer mandates are based on multiple payers. Current private insurers would continue to compete and sell their insurance goods in the private market, although they would face more government regulations. Second, many proposals of this group include incremental exemptions and subsidies for small or new businesses, part-time workers, and nonworkers to make insurance available to them. Third, some proposals involve expanding Medicaid or a similar public back-up program to cover the unemployed and those whose employers preferred to pay the tax rather than provide coverage. Finally, most recent employer mandate reforms incorporate managed competition[22] and managed care into a global budget system in an attempt to achieve cost control.

Tax Credit Approach: Another group of proposals includes the use of tax credits and vouchers to expand access to health care coverage. The tax credit approach was advocated by the Bush administration, which proposed creating new tax credits and deductions to encourage individuals to buy insurance coverage. The Bush plan includes no expansion of public insurance programs, no mandate on employers to provide insurance to their employees, and no mandates on consumers to purchase insurance polices. Rather, the plan tries to induce individuals to buy health coverage by subsidizing the purchase of insurance through tax credits or deductions. Under the Bush plan, a tax credit or deduction would be tailored to income and family size.[23] The credit or deduction would be reduced by any amount that an employer contributes to an employee's health insurance. Persons covered by other public health programs would not be eligible. The Bush plan limits the tax credit only to the purchase of health insurance. In addition, the Bush plan includes other provisions such as insurance market reform to protect small groups, health risk pools, malpractice reform, and the use of managed care to contain costs (Silow-Carroll, 1993, pp.146-147).

          Another plan proposed by Pauly et al. (1991) involves tax credits but also more government requirements for coverage and benefit packages. Under this proposal, every person would be required to obtain basic coverage, through either an individual or a family insurance plan. To support the purchase of coverage, the federal government would establish refundable tax credits (effectively, vouchers for persons with no tax liability). The credit would correspond to the premium for the required coverage and would be inversely related to a family's income. The credit also would be adjusted to reflect each family's risk category. All insurance plans would be required to provide at least the minimum benefits specified by the government including basic acute care services and a set of preventive services. In addition, insurance plans could not require deductibles, copayments, or maximum out-of-pocket payments in excess of the levels specified by the federal government (levels which would depend on the policyholder's family income). Under Pauly's plan, current tax exemptions for 100% of employer's contributions and 25% of premiums paid by the self-employed would be eliminated, and Medicaid and Medicare would be gradually phased into the new system (Pauly et al., 1991, pp.10-11).

          The central theme that distinguishes the tax credit approach from the other approaches is a primary emphasis on minimal disruption of existing payment and delivery mechanisms. This approach is based on the notion that the strengths of the current system outweigh its defects, and thus the goal of reform should focus on making a good system better. To control costs and expand access, this reform relies on pluralistic and voluntary efforts within the private sector, rather than governmental regulatory efforts. Most proposals include incremental strategies such as small market reform; streamlined billing and claims processing procedures; malpractice reform; and incentives for expansion of innovative, integrated managed care systems on a capitated basis. These strategies contrast with the global budgets, price controls, and insurance mandates often seen in proposals with regulatory emphases. While the first two groups of proposals (i.e., the single payer and the employer mandate approaches) contain a mixture of market and regulatory reforms, the tax credit approach is closest to the market end of the spectrum. (Lewin, 1993, p.13).

Notes

1. See, for example, Okun (1975).

2. The 1962 amendments required that the states deduct work-related expenses from earnings before reducing benefits.

3. For example, the Supported Work Demonstration (from 1975 to 1979), and the Employment Opportunity Pilot Projects (from 1979 to 1981) were notable programs conducted under the Ford and Carter Administrations (Garfinkel and McLanahan, 1986, pp.116-117).

4. In addition to the workfare provision, OBRA included AFDC budget cuts. Under OBRA, welfare benefits to working mothers were cut substantially. The work incentive provision in AFDC that had disregarded the first $30 of earnings plus a third earned in excess of $30 per month was reduced from eight to four months. Individually determined work-related expense deductions with no maximum were replaced by standard deductions of $50 for part-time work and $75 for full-time work per month. Furthermore, OBRA made families with gross incomes in excess of 150% of the state's need standard ineligible for benefits. The later legislation in 1984 liberalized some of these benefit cuts: the $30 set aside was extended from four to twelve months; the $75 a month deduction for work-related expenses was applied to part-time as well as full-time work; and the eligibility level for people already on welfare was increased from 150% to 185% of the state's need standard (Garfinkel and McLanahan, 1986, p.133).

5. The Reagan Administration proposed that states require AFDC mothers to work for their relief checks in community work experience programs. But Congress passed legislation that permitted states to do so (implying that states were not required) (Garfinkel and McLanahan, 1986, p.134).

6. For example, Employment and Training (ET) Choices in Massachusetts, Greater Avenues for Independence (GAIN) in California, Realizing Economic Achievement (REACH) in New Jersey, and the Family Independence Program (FIP) in the state of Washington.

7.Federal involvement in private child support enforcement actually began in the 1950s, but it never became a prominent issue until the 1975 Amendment. See Katz (1982) for a detailed history.

8.In addition to Medicaid, as part of the War on Poverty in 1965, the federal government funded a small demonstration project called 'neighborhood health centers,' whose goal was to provide community-based care to poor people. By 1975 these programs received their own legislative authority and were renamed 'community health centers.' Also during the Democratic administration of the 1960s, federally funded maternal and child health and family planning programs were expanded (Levitan, 1990).

9.When inflation is considered, as a result, federal funding for maternal and child health programs and community health centers decreased by 32% between 1978 and 1984, and Medicaid spending per child declined by 13%. See Sardell (1990), pp.279-280.

10.For taxpayers with two or more children, the credit is reduced by 12.36 cents per each dollar.

11.The pilot program in Wisconsin included two other components: wage subsidy and a surtax on custodial parents who receive a public subsidy. See Garfinkel, Robins, Wong, & Meyer (1990).

12.There are other versions of CSAS. Some of these proposed assured benefits available for all custodial parents and those on AFDC as well.

13.For an overall review of programs in these nations, see Table 8 (pp. 60-72) of Vadakin (1968).

14.Vadakin (1968) reported that among sixty-two countries which had children's allowances in a broad sense, fourteen countries had a universal system and the remaining forty-eight nations had an employment-related system.

15.In addition to residence, eligibility may require school attendance.

16.See Center for National Health Program Studies (1992); Grumbach et al. (1991); and Himmelstein & Woolhandler (1989).

17.See Mitchell (1991).

18.Those below the poverty line would not pay any premium, whereas those between 100% and 200% of poverty would pay on a graduated basis. Workers whose employers 'pay' would pay just 20% of the actuarial value of coverage.

19.See Bill Clinton for President Committee (1992).

20.Under Clinton's proposal, Medicaid would continue, which is another difference from the Mitchell bill.

21.These features are cited from CNHPS (1992), p.120.

22.The concept of managed competition was originally developed by the 'Jackson Hole Group' led by Stanford University economist E. Enthoven and Interstudy P. Ellwood, M.D. Managed competition would band employers and individuals into large cooperatives to purchase health insurance, giving small businesses and individuals the same bargaining power as large companies. Providers -- doctors, hospitals, and insurers -- would form partnerships that would compete for the cooperatives' business, each trying to offer the best-quality, most cost effective health plan (Lewin, 1993, pp.8-12).

23.People with incomes below the tax-filing threshold would receive the maximum tax credit of $1250 for single persons, $2500 for married couples, and $3750 for families of three or more. The credit would be scaled down as income rises, decreasing to 10 percent of the maximum credit at an income of 150 percent of the tax-filing threshold. Those with incomes above 150 percent of the threshold and below the eligibility limits could take either the partial credit ($125, $250, or $375) or a deduction of up to $1250, $2500, or $3750, depending on family size (Silow-Carroll, 1993).

III

Literature Review

This chapter will review previous research findings regarding programs for child support assurance, children's allowance, and national health insurance, focusing primarily on simulation analysis for the costs and economic effects of the proposals.

Prior Research on Child Support Assurance System

Expected Impact of Child Support Assurance System (CSAS): If CSAS is fully implemented, Meyer, Garfinkel, Robins, and Oellerich (1991a) predict the following effects: (a) CSAS will increase the number of families with child support awards, particularly because of the incentive that the assured benefit is available only to those with awards; (b) the uniform standard will increase the dollar amounts of awards; (c) immediate income withholding will increase child support payments and thus the percentage of awards collected; (d) poverty among custodial parent families will decrease through increased private child support and the assured benefit; (e) CSAS will increase the number of hours worked by AFDC custodial parents, while it is expected to decrease the number of hours worked by non-AFDC custodial parents; and (f) CSAS will decrease AFDC recipiency as a result of the increase in labor supply among AFDC custodial parents (pp. 8-11). In addition, a reduction in AFDC participation will subsequently decrease food stamps and Medicaid caseloads because of their categorical entitlement linked to AFDC.

The effect of CSAS on the labor supply and AFDC recipiency is based on the static economic theory. Meyer et al. (1991a) particularly suggest the following theoretical reason for the direction of their prediction: "given time and budget constraints, individuals consider the amount of income and leisure they would receive from all possible hours of work, and select the amount of work that maximizes their utility. In the absence of the AFDC program, any increase in unearned income through private child support and assured benefit will decrease the labor supply of custodial parents, partly because they can achieve the same amount of total income as before while working fewer hours. The labor supply model becomes complicated especially for poor female heads of household with children who are typically given an option of whether to participate in AFDC. For this group, their labor supply decision is made simultaneously with considering welfare participation. Thus, single women with children are assumed to consider two potential alternatives, whether to be on AFDC or to participate in CSAS and work, and then to select the option that provides the highest utility" (pp. 8-9).[1]

In choosing the highest utility, we should remember that the assured benefit of CSAS is not income-tested and that the AFDC benefit is income-tested, which means that the implicit tax rates of AFDC are higher than for CSAS. In other words, custodial parents get more return from work under CSAS than under AFDC. It is thus predicted that CSAS will induce an increase in hours of work for AFDC custodial parents.[2]

In brief, labor supply theory predicts that CSAS will decrease the labor supply of non-AFDC custodial parents, while it will increase the labor supply of AFDC custodial parents and consequently decrease AFDC participation (i.e., earnings through work combined with the assured benefit may provide enough income so that a mother is able to leave AFDC). However, the net effect of CSAS on the labor supply for all families is an empirical question, depending on the distribution of families along the budget sets.

In addition to its effect on the labor supply, Meyer et al. (1991a) also suggest other possible reasons for CSAS decreasing AFDC caseloads (p.11). First, for some women, increased private child support alone (due to CSAS implementation) may provide more income than welfare, and thus they will be able to exit AFDC. Second, the assured benefit may be greater than the AFDC maximum benefit in some states, and women with awards living in those states will choose to move off AFDC, although they may not work. The final possibility is related to preferences rather than utility counts. The authors suggest that "there may eventually be a change in community values that has a feedback effect: dependence on child support rather than on AFDC may become the norm for single parents, and this may further decrease welfare participation." (p.11).[3]

Although the predicted direction of the effects of CSAS is theoretically clear, their empirical magnitude is uncertain. Much research has been conducted to estimate those possible effects of CSAS. The more important question from a policy standpoint is: what would be the costs and benefits of CSAS when CSAS is fully implemented and all plausible effects are taken into account? CSAS initially requires a certain amount of costs to pay assured benefits to custodial families whose noncustodial parents pay less than the assured level. At the same time, CSAS is expected to collect more private child support payments and also expected to bring some public savings from welfare benefit expenditures through decreased welfare participation including AFDC, food stamps, and Medicaid. In addition, changes in the labor supply behavior of custodial parents should result in a change in income tax revenue. When greater collection of child support, savings of welfare expenditures, and the change in income taxes are all counted together, what is the net cost to the government? Since CSAS will affect the incomes of all custodial families, what will be resulting impact on the incidence of poverty and income distribution under CSAS reform? How much loss of efficiency will be incurred due to an addition of this public subsidy? These policy-directed questions can be answered by cost and benefit analysis through simulation research. Of the broad range of studies related to CSAS, this literature review will focus primarily on simulation research estimating its costs and benefits.

Previous Estimates of Child Support Assurance: Three empirical studies provide simulations of a national CSAS: Lerman (1989); Meyer, Garfinkel, Robins, and Oellerich (1991a); and Congressional Budget Office (1992). Lerman (1989), based on the Survey of Incomes and Program Participation (SIPP), simulated four different plans: the Wisconsin CSAS with an assured benefit of $3000 a year for the first child and a surtax on the custodial parent's earnings; a lower assured benefit of $1080 a year available only for custodial parents with awards; a lower benefit of $1080 but available for all custodial parents; and a combined plan of $1080 assured benefit (available for all custodial parents) and $1080 refundable tax credit (for a family of mother and two kids) that would replace the $2000 personal exemption for children. According to Lerman's estimates, CSAS reduces the poverty gap by 2% ($1080 assured benefit restricted to those awarded) to 45% (assurance combined with credit); it also reduces the poverty rate by 1% to 19%. AFDC participation is estimated to a decrease from 4% ($1080 assured benefit to those awarded) to 30% (combined plan).[4] Finally, the gross costs of Lerman's plans are estimated to be from $2.4 billion (for the restricted assurance of $1080) to $8.5 billion (for the assured benefit combined with tax credit). After subtracting the reduction in AFDC outlays, the net costs in 1985 dollars are estimated in a range from $1.1 billion (for the assured benefit of $1080 restricted) to $3.6 billion (assured benefit of $1080 available for all). In Lerman's simulation, however, a few things should be noted: he did not simulate increases in the percentage with awards or the percentage collected; he did not allow labor supply responses; and AFDC underreporting was not corrected.

Research by Meyer, Garfinkel, Robins, and Oellerich (1991a) provides estimates for the national CSAS by using the 1986 Current Population Survey (CPS). Meyer et al.(1991a) simulated three different assured benefit levels: $1000, $2000, and $3000 for the first child year, each level with the benefit increased by $1000 for the second child, $1000 for the third, $500 for the fourth, and $500 for the fifth or more. Since the program cost of CSAS critically depends on private child support payments, the authors simulated each level of these assured plans under four different scenarios for changes in award rate, award level, and collections. Other features in their simulation were that assured benefits were limited to custodial parents with awards; eligible parents were required to choose either AFDC or the assured benefit; changes in the labor supply of custodial parents in response to CSAS reform were allowed; public portions of assured benefit were treated as taxable income; and the AFDC underreporting problem was corrected.

According to Meyer et al.'s estimates, CSAS reduces the poverty gap by 2% (at the $1000 assured level under no improvement in child support) to 39% (at the $3000 level under perfect child support system), but its impact on the poverty rate is less, ranging from 1% (at the $1000 under no improvement) to 20% (at the $3000 under perfect system). The effects of CSAS on AFDC participation are also sensitive to the assured levels and child support scenarios assumed. CSAS decreases AFDC caseloads by 3% (at the $1000 under no improvement) to 50% (at the $3000 under the perfect system). As a result, CSAS is predicted to save AFDC outlays from $100 million to

$4.8 billion in 1985 dollars. As for its effects on labor supply behavior, CSAS discourages work by non-AFDC custodial parents but not significantly, reaching at most to only a 6% decline even at the highest level ($3000) under the perfect system. However, CSAS is estimated to increase the hours worked by AFDC parents substantially, ranging from 4% (at the $1000 under the no improvement) to 74% (at the $3000 under the perfect system). Their estimates for program cost are in a somewhat broad range. CSAS would require a gross cost in 1985 dollar figures between $197 million (at the $1000 assured benefit under no improvement in award and collection rates) and $5.9 billion (at the $3000 under the no improvement). After counting AFDC savings, additional income tax revenue from taxing assured benefits, and income tax changes due to labor supply changes, CSAS is estimated at the range between a net cost of $4.2 billion and a savings of $2.8 billion.

Most recently, the Congressional Budget Office staff released its cost estimates for the CSAS program. CBO (1992) simulated a bit different CSAS program with two new components for an incentive purpose: supplementary payment and AFDC incentive payment. To supplement the absent parent's child support payment and reward custodial parents for the payment, a supplementary payment was made to all families who received child support payments, which was set equal to 50% of child support payment up to a maximum of $1200 a year. The CBO staff also proposed to replace current child support disregard of $50 with an AFDC incentive payment (the same amount, but available for all AFDC custodial mothers with awards) in order to induce custodial parents to seek awards. For levels of assurance, four plans were simulated: (1) an assured benefit of $1500 for one child, $2000 for two, $2300 for three, $2500 for four or more children; (2) $2250 for one child, $3000 for two, $3500 for three, and $3850 for four or more children; (3) a benefit set to the lesser of the first plan or the family's child support award; and (4) a benefit set to the lesser of the second plan or the family's child support award. For child support variables, the CBO simulated two alternatives by employing reported amounts of child support and reported amounts of award level under an assumption of full collections. Like Lerman (1989), they also simulated two options in eligibility: first, assured benefits were restricted only to those with awards; second, benefits were available to all custodial parents. As a difference from other studies, however, the CBO simulation allowed assured benefits available to AFDC custodial parents. Similar to Lerman (1989) but different from Meyer et al.(1991a), labor supply responses and AFDC underreporting were ignored, and assured benefits were not taxed.

   The CBO staff presents two sets of results, one with CSAS only and the other with both CSAS and two payment plans (supplemental and AFDC incentive payments). By CBO estimates, an assured benefit would require a gross cost between $1.7 billion and $17 billion depending on eligibility criteria, assured guarantee level, and child support assumed to be collected. AFDC savings due to CSAS also are predicted as between $0.4 billion and $4.5 billion in 1989 dollars. The estimated net cost of the assured benefit, defined as the gross cost less the AFDC savings, is estimated ranging from $1.3 billion to $5.4 billion (depending on guarantee level and the assumption of child support payment) if assured benefits are limited to families with awards. The net cost increases to between $5.9 billion and $12.6 billion if assured benefits are available to all parents. Unfortunately, the CBO's estimates do not provide much information about other effects, such as on poverty or AFDC participation.

   It is difficult to compare the estimated costs and effects of CSAS from different studies, because there are a variety of possible causes for the different estimates in the simulations. Table 3-1 presents differences in the features of CSAS as simulated in three studies. In order to compare the results from these studies, the most comparable plan from each simulation study is selected; the estimated costs and effects of CSAS under the selected plans are presented in Table 3-2. In Table 3-2, the assured level of $1000 estimated by Meyer et al.(1991a) is comparable with Lerman's plan of $1080 in that both simulations assume no improvement in child support, limit the assured benefit to those with awards, and the dollar amount of assurance is very close. The effects on AFDC caseloads and poverty are almost identical in these two studies: a 3-4% reduction in AFDC caseloads, and 1% and 2% declines in the poverty rate and poverty gap, respectively. But Lerman's estimate of net cost is higher than that of Meyer et al.(a difference of $0.7 billion) probably because changes in income tax revenue resulting from labor supply responses and from taxing assured benefits are counted into the calculation of net cost in Meyer et al. A higher level of assurance ($3000 level) is also comparable between Meyer et al. and Lerman studies. This level provides a decline of 14% (Meyer et al.) versus 12% (Lerman) in AFDC caseloads; a decrease of 9% (Meyer et al.) versus 4% (Lerman) in the poverty gap; and a net cost of $2.2 billion (Meyer et al.) versus $1.6 billion (Lerman), all indicating that Meyer et al. estimate higher effects and lower costs than Lerman. This difference may have resulted from Lerman charging a surtax on custodial earnings for his Wisconsin CSAS simulation, while Meyer et al. did not.

Since the CBO's estimates do not present percent changes in AFDC caseloads and poverty, only AFDC savings and program costs can be compared with the other studies. The CBO plan of $2250 can be compared with the $2000 assured benefit of Meyer et al.: AFDC savings of $1.4 billion (CBO) versus $0.4 billion (Meyer et al.); a gross cost of $6.8 billion (CBO) versus $2.5 billion (Meyer et al.); and a net cost of $5.4 billion (CBO) versus $1.8 billion (Meyer et al.). Because dollar figures are stated for different years (1989 dollars in CBO and 1985 dollars in Meyer et al.), these costs are not directly comparable. However, with inflation taken into account, the CBO's net cost is estimated at 2.6 times higher than that of Meyer et al. Among many possible sources for this difference, one primary source may be the different definition of net cost. The CBO defines it as the gross cost minus the AFDC savings, while Meyer et al. counted other savings (e.g., tax collections from public benefits) besides the AFDC savings into the net cost.

Limitations of Previous Research on Child Support Assurance: The previous studies have several limitations in their estimates. Lerman's (1989) analysis does not consider an improvement in award incidence and in award levels, both of which are likely to occur as a result of the Family Support Act as well as the elements of CSAS itself. The Lerman study also ignores changes in labor supply behaviors, although some change in hours of work is expected among custodial parents in response to increased private child support or to an assured benefit. In addition, AFDC underreporting of the data (SIPP) has not been corrected. According to one report, AFDC recipiency in the SIPP data are underreported by 37% (Marquis and Moore, 1989). The CBO estimation (1992) also has similar limitations: labor supply responses and AFDC underreporting (in the CPS data) are ignored; an improvement in the percentage of custodial parents with awards and in award levels is not considered; and, except for costs and AFDC savings, the other effects of CSAS (for example, on incomes, poverty, income distribution) are not estimated. The AFDC underreporting problem in these two studies might lead to understating a decline in

AFDC recipiency or the amount of AFDC savings, and thus to overstating the net cost of CSAS.

On the other hand, the Meyer et al. study (1991a) complements these listed limitations in many ways: the study incorporates the labor supply model to estimate a change in hours of work in response to the reform; AFDC underreporting in the CPS data has been corrected; and several possible changes in private child support situations are tested by simulating four scenarios (from the worst case to the most optimistic case). However, the Meyer et al. analysis (along with all other studies) still has several problems. First, neither Medicaid nor food stamps are considered in simulation. Given the current links of both Medicaid and food stamps to AFDC recipiency, ignoring Medicaid and food stamps may lead to overestimating the number of families that would leave AFDC rolls under CSAS. If a benefit package of Medicaid and food stamps along with AFDC is considered, there would be a large break in the budget line at the break-even point, which means that an exit from welfare at this point would decrease income. In the Meyer et al. study, as a result, the estimate of a 2% to 50% decline in AFDC caseloads may be somewhat overstated. The second problem in the Meyer et al. study (and in the CBO study as well) is associated with the data employed rather than simulation itself. Both studies employ the CPS data from different years. The CPS data has undercounted the number of families eligible for child support for three reasons: (a) the data missed mothers who had no children from the most recent divorce or separation but had children from an earlier divorce or separation; (b) the data did not include mothers who are currently married but had children out of wedlock; and (c) the CPS data did not include custodial fathers. This undercount in the CPS data would primarily result in underestimating the gross cost of CSAS. The direction of potential bias for the net cost, due to these two problems, is ambiguous. Certainly, if estimated AFDC savings are overstated and the predicted gross cost is understated, both together would result in an under-estimated net cost in the Meyer et al. study. However, considering Medicaid and food stamps would result in some savings in their outlays. Including this savings in the calculation of net costs would push the underestimate somewhat upward, but we don't know how much.

Table 3-1
Features Of Prior CSAS Simulations

CSAS	Meyer et.al	Lerman	CBO
Data	1986 CPS: 1985 yr	1984 SIPP: 1985 yr	1990 CPS: 1989 yr
Child Support Assumed	- current payments - current award and collection rates w/ percentage standard - medium improvement in award and collection rates w/ percentage standard - 100% awards and collections w/ percentage standard	- current payments - current award and collection rates w/ percentage standard for Wisconsin plan	- current payments - full payments of current awards
Who eligible?	- those w/ awards	- those w/ awards - all parents	- those w/ awards - all parents
Level of Assurance /1st Child	- $1000 - $2000 - $3000	- $1080 - $3000 of WI CSAS	- $1500 - $2250 - two others
Both CSAS and AFDC	No	No	Yes
Surtax	No	Yes only for WI CSAS	No
Labor Supply	Yes	No	No
Benefits Taxed	Yes	No	No
AFDC Adjusted	Yes	No	No
Other Elements	None	Tax credit ($1080)	Incentive Payments

Table 3-2
Comparison Of Previous Estimates For CSAS

	%Chg AFDC Cases	AFDC Savings $bill	%Chg Pov Rate	%Chg Pov Gap	Gross Cost $bill	Net Cost $bill
Meyer et. al (no improvement) : 1985 yr						
$1000	-3	.1	-1	-2	.6	.4
$2000	-8	.4	-3	-5	2.5	1.8
$3000	-13	.8	-6	-9	5.9	4.2
$3000 * w/ pct standard	-14	1.0	-6	-9	3.4	2.2
Lerman: 1985 yr						
$1080 [b] current CS	-4	?	-1	-2	?	1.1
$3000 [c] (WI)	-12	?	-3	-4	?	1.6
CBO (current child support): 1989 yr						
$1500	?	.9	?	?	4.0	3.1
$2250	?	1.4	?	?	6.8	5.4

Notes:
[a] Award levels equal to the percentage standard, but no improvement in award and collection rates assumed.
[b] Current child support payment assumed.
[c] Award level equal to the percentage standard, but current award and collection rates assumed.

Prior Research on Children's Allowance

During the late 1960s, several proposals for children's allowances were made, and some estimates of their costs and antipoverty effects were suggested. Schorr (1966) proposed two alternative plans, one of which was to provide a preschool allowance of $600 a year for every child under age 6. The plan was proposed to be financed out of general revenue, with tax exemptions for children to be eliminated, and allowances to be taxable. According his estimates using 1964 figures, the gross cost would amount to $14.9 billion and the net cost to $5.9 billion, with $9 billion recaptured through tax collections by wiping out exemptions and by taxing allowances. Schorr further estimated that about one half of the families with children under six would be brought out of poverty by a program of preschool allowances (Schorr, 1966, p.153).

Another proposal for a children's allowance, suggested by Vadakin (1968), would pay $120 per year for every child in the family under the age of 18, regardless of income or employment status, but on the condition of school attendance. The program was to be financed from general tax revenues of the federal government. Benefit payments were to be included as taxable income, but tax exemptions for children were to continue. For this proposal, Vadakin estimated a gross cost of $8.6 billion for the year 1968, including administrative expenses. From that amount, according to his estimate, $1.3 billion would be recovered through the income tax on benefits, leaving a net annual cost at $7.3 billion (Vadakin, 1968, p.188). By using the income data of 1965, the author further estimated that the program would increase the incomes of families with earnings less than $3000 per year by 12% for families with three children, by 16% for families with four children, and by at least 20% for those with five children (Vadakin, 1968, p.190).

Orshansky (1968), in preparation for the Children's Allowances Conference in 1967 that was sponsored by the Citizens' Committee for Children, put together various schemes for a children's allowance and presented the expected costs and antipoverty effects. Orshansky considered several optional programs, including $300 and $600 (per year) plans for every child under age 18, $300 and $600 plans limited only to the third and subsequent children under age 18, a plan with $600 to children under age 6 and $120 to children aged 6-17, and a tapered allowance plan.[5] In all plans, Orshansky proposed to eliminate tax exemptions for children and to count benefits as taxable income. Based on 1965 data, gross costs were estimated from $6.7 billion to $41.2 billion; net costs were in the range of $4.1 billion to $28.5 billion. These plans were expected to reduce the number of poor families with children by 15.2% to 64.3%, depending on the plan.[6]

Musgrave, Heller, and Peterson (1970) also simulated a variant of children's allowance--the demo-grant plan--to compare its cost effectiveness with a negative income tax (NIT) plan on the basis of target efficiency. These proposed demo-grant plans included allowances per adult as well as per child, with payments made independently of income level but dependent on family size. Under the plan, payments were to be taxable and personal tax exemptions were to be repealed.[7] At the middle level of budget constraints,[8] grants were set to $266 per adult and $133 per child. For a comparison, the authors also simulated several NIT plans, one of which included a 50% tax rate and a minimum guarantee at 67% of the poverty line. Using the 1966 Survey of Economic Opportunity data, the poverty gap was reduced by $4.8 billion under the demo-grant plan and $11.4 billion under the NIT, given the same net cost of $14.5 billion in 1966 figures. The number of families in poverty was decreased by 2.1 million under the demo-grant plan and 4.5 million under the NIT. By these criteria, the authors concluded that the NIT was superior to the demo-grant plan.[9]

More recently, several scholars have again proposed to replace current tax exemptions for children with a children's allowance. Garfinkel and McLanahan (1986) suggest that a child exemption of $2000 would be converted to a children's allowance of $300 to $400 a year per child at no extra cost (p.183). Ellwood (1988) also has estimated that the current income tax deduction could be converted at no net cost to a roughly $500 children's allowance (p.118). However, neither of these authors measured the effects of their proposals.

More elaborate estimates on the costs and effects of children allowances based on micro-data simulation have been provided by Meyer, Phillips, and Maritato (1991b). In their proposal, the income tax deductions for children would be replaced with a universal children's allowance for each unmarried child who is currently eligible to receive the tax deduction. The program would be funded out of general revenues and the monthly benefits would be considered non-taxable income for the income tax code but unearned income for the purpose of AFDC benefit counts. Three levels of children's allowance would be determined in the following way: (a) an allowance of $292 a year per child which would be cost-neutral with the elimination of current tax exemptions for children; (b) a level of $312 which was arrived at by incorporating any savings (AFDC and food stamps savings) that would result from the first level of allowance; and (c) a higher level of allowance set to $1000 per year per child (Meyer et al., 1991, p.471).

Using the Survey of Income and Program Participation (1984 SIPP panel), the authors estimated that the program would reduce the number of families with children in poverty by 2.6% under the lowest level ($292), 2.8% under the middle level ($312), and 14.6% under the highest level ($1000). The program also would decrease the poverty gap by 6.4% (lowest), 7% (middle), and 24% (highest). As for its effects on income distribution, the children's allowance was expected to push some families out of the bottom level of the income distribution. The cost-neutral plan of $312 would decrease the number of families with very low incomes (less than half of the poverty line) by more than 6%, while the larger allowance of $1000 would decrease the number by more than 25% (Meyer et al., 1991b, Table 2).

Meyer, Phillips, and Maritato (1991b) also estimated the impact of children's allowance on welfare participation and labor supply. According to the authors, an allowance of $312 would decrease AFDC caseloads by 7.1% and food stamp participation by less than 1%. The plan of $1000 would decrease the number of AFDC families by 24% and food stamp recipients by 4%. The authors also predicted that aggregate changes in labor supply were quite small for non-AFDC groups. Even with the highest allowance, the average annual hours worked by men decreased by only 3 hours (0.2% decline) and the average annual hours of women not on AFDC decreased by just 2 hours (0.2% decline). However, it was predicted that allowances would increase the labor supply of women on AFDC. The authors indicated that the average hours worked by women originally receiving AFDC would increase from 2.1% to 13.9%, depending on the level of allowance (Meyer et al., 1991b, Table 3). Finally, regarding gross costs using 1989 dollar figures, the allowance of $292 would require a gross cost of $22 billion, and the $312 level would incur a gross cost of $23.4 billion incorporating the federal welfare savings of $1.4 billion. As mentioned earlier, however, these two levels of allowance were set as cost-neutral. The $1000 allowance, according to the authors, would require $76 billion in benefits being paid out, with a net cost of $49 billion to the federal government (Meyer et al., 1991b, Table 1).

Some limitations are found in these previous studies of children's allowance. First of all, except for Orshansky (1968), Musgrave et al.(1970), and Meyer, Phillips, and Maritato (1991b), most studies did not mention the data sources from which their estimates were derived, leaving the possibility that aggregate data might have been employed. Not surprisingly, such studies did not present much information on estimated effects other than cost estimates.

Second, all studies except the most recent (Meyer et al. [1991b]) did not consider behavior changes in response to a children's allowance program. Ignoring labor supply responses could be misleading. For example, Musgrave et al.(1970) arrived at the conclusion that the NIT was superior to the demo-grant plan, based on their analysis model which disregarded the effects of tax rates on work efforts. In their analysis, the advantages of NIT were obtained at the cost of a 50% marginal tax rate against a 15% marginal tax rate under demo-grant plans.[10] If this substantial difference in tax rates and their effects on labor supply could be allowed for, the picture might be different.

Compared to other studies, Meyer et al.(1991b) employed a much more sophisticated model which incorporated the changes in welfare participation and labor supply. The authors also used the micro data rather than the aggregate data, which gave their estimates another advantage. However, there are still a few shortcomings in their simulation model. As indicated for CSAS estimates in the previous section, first, the authors ignored Medicaid values in the prediction of AFDC participation and labor supply. This may have resulted in overstated reduction of AFDC caseloads (and also AFDC savings), and thus the understated estimates of net cost. Second, the authors did not incorporate the financing schedule for the cost-incurring plan of $1000. Families with low incomes may be required to pay some part of costs depending on the shape of financing schedule. When the financing scheme is ignored, the estimated impacts on income distribution (or perhaps on poverty) could be biased in some way. All the other studies have this limitation as well.

Prior Research on National Health Insurance

Prior research on the effects of health care reform covers a broad range of issues including the impact on macro economy, employment and wages, insurance markets, consumers, and so on. My literature review primarily focuses on empirical studies of costs and redistributional effects.

Estimated Costs and Shifts in Financial Burden: Most prior empirical studies have been directed to estimate the costs of the proposal and any shift in financial burdens among different sectors (i.e., who bears the costs)--the government, the group of employers, and the group of individuals. Those estimated costs are in a broad range, depending on the inclusiveness of coverage, comprehensiveness of benefits, financing method, and strategy of cost containment. Table 3-3 presents a summary of existing cost estimates by some classified proposals (this table is adapted from Lewin, 1993).

The first column shows the net costs estimated from single payer proposals, ranging from a decrease of $26 billion to an increase of $30 billion. Variations in cost estimates are related to differences in the basic benefit package, administrative costs, utilization changes, and methodology (Lewin, 1993, p.10). Most costs (or savings) under this type of proposal are likely to shift from private sectors to the government. For proposals that call for a 'straight' employer mandate, the increase in national health care expenditures is estimated between $10 and $15 billion (second column): the net cost to employers is predicted from $12 to $86 billion; the cost to the government would decrease by $8 billion; and the cost to individuals would also decrease by the range of $5 to $14 billion. Variations in coverage and cost estimates shown in the second column are a result of proposals excluding certain employers or employees, differences in the basic benefit packages, and methodology (Lewin, 1992, p.10). The third column includes employer mandate proposals with 'play or pay' options: the cost to employers ranges from $30 to $45 billion; the cost to the government between $18 and $37 billion; and the cost to individuals from $1 to $8 billion. Similarly, the broad range of these estimates is a result of the size of the payroll tax, the presence of subsidies for small employers, and methodology (Lewin, 1993, p.10). The sixth column presents cost estimates from tax credit proposals, indicating a range of $4 billion savings to $20 billion cost to the government. Again, the range of estimates depends on the size and availability of tax credits for individuals, and whether or not employers are required to participate (Lewin, 1993, p.10). All these estimates indicate that the single payer plan would bring the largest shift of costs to the government, but under employer mandate plans, most of the financing burden would fall on employers.

Some studies analyzed the cost issue from a different angle. The Congressional Budget Office (CBO, 1991) estimated changes in national health expenditures under the single-payer system and the all-payer system. A major focus of this study was to compare different types of health care systems with respect to costs. Under both systems, the CBO study assumed universal coverage and the use of current Medicare payment rates for providers. One difference between systems is that the single payer system involved a single public insurer, a uniform benefit package and tax financing, while the all-payer system had the current mix of private and public insurers, current mixed packages (but the Medicare package assumed for the uninsured), and mixed financing of premiums (by the insured and employers) and taxes. The CBO (1991) study reported that national health spending (using a mid-range of assumption) would decrease by $26.3 billion (1989 dollars) under the single-payer system, but increase by $5.6 billion under the all-payer system, indicating that the single-payer system is more effective for cost control than the all-payer system. Also, according to the study, the single payer system would require a cost of $143.6 billion to the government, but bring a savings of $170 billion to the private sector. On the other hand, the all-payer system would imply much less cost to the government ($25.6 billion), and much less savings to the private sector ($20 billion) (see Table 11 of Congress Budget Office, 1991). In the CBO study, the difference in cost estimates was largely due to a difference in administrative costs under the two different systems.

Related to the cost issue, a number of studies[11] have been concerned about the potential savings of national health insurance on administrative costs. Most of these studies employed a Canadian-style single-payer system or a Medicare model to estimate administrative savings. Estimated savings on providers' overhead costs under a single-payer system range from 0% to 13.1% as a percent of personal health care expenditures, and savings on insurers' overhead costs are estimated in the range of 4.2% to 5.4% of personal health care expenditures.

Redistributional Impact: Although any type of proposal would reshape the distribution of health benefits and health care financing for different income classes, empirical analysis of redistributional effects has been rarely produced. Very recently, Zedlewski, Holahan, Blumberg, and Winterbottom (1993) analyzed the distributional effects of alternative health care proposals. This study compared four alternative plans: two plans of single payer system (one with cost sharing and the other without cost sharing), and two types of employer mandate (one for straight mandate and the other for play-or-pay mandate).

In Zedlewski et al. (1993)'s simulation, the single payer plan with cost sharing provides first dollar coverage to all individuals below the poverty line, and phases in full cost sharing between 100% and 200% of poverty. Under the cost-sharing plan, the nonpoor are responsible for a deductible of $200 per person and 20% coinsurance. The plan without cost sharing does not require any deductible or copayment, regardless of income levels. The new revenue necessary to finance either single payer plan is raised by increases in income and payroll taxes in this simulation (pp.100-103).

Under employer mandates in Zedlewski et al.'s simulation, employers are required to provide a basic benefit plan (the same benefit package as under single payer systems) to all full-time workers and their dependents. Under both straight and play-or-pay types, the employer share of premiums is set at 80% of worker premium cost and 40% of dependent costs. Under the play-or-pay plan, an employer is allowed to choose to pay a 7% payroll tax instead of the required premium share. Both types of employer mandate plan require individuals who are neither full-time workers nor the dependents of workers to buy into a publicly sponsored insurance plan. The same cost sharing scheme of the single payer systems is assumed under employer mandates (pp.113-119).[12]

By using the 1990 Current Population Survey, Zedlewski et al. conclude that all simulated plans would redistribute income from the upper to the low income classes, and that such redistribution would be greater under single payer systems than under employer mandate plans. Under the current system, according to the authors, individuals in the lowest quintile spend 13% of income plus noncash compensation.[13]

Assuming strong cost containment, this percentage under the single
payer system would be cut down more than half--5.1% (no cost
sharing) and 5.8% (cost sharing); and under employer mandates, the
percentage would go down slightly--about 10% and 11% under the
play-or-pay plan and straight mandate plan, respectively. On the other
hand, for individuals in the top 10% of income distribution, health
spending as a percent of income would increase from 8.2% (current)
to the range of 11% to 12% under the single payer plan depending on
cost sharing; and almost no change (8.5%) under employer mandates.
The authors further present percent changes in income less health
financing and other taxes by income classes. Under single payer
systems, families in the lowest quintile would increase average income
after health spending by around 10%, and those in the top 10% of
distribution would decrease income by 2-5% depending on cost sharing
and assumptions employed. Under employer mandates, the lowest
quintile would increase income by 3-4%, while the highest quintile
would slightly decrease by less than 1.5%.

Another study (in spite of its 1970s estimates) evaluated the
redistributional impact of national insurance plans. Davis (1975)
compared especially the administration plan (similar to employer
mandate)[14] with the Kennedy-Mills plan (similar to single payer
plan).[15] The study focused on an analysis of the costs ultimately borne
by individuals and the distribution of that cost among people of
different income classes. The study indicated that about 22% of the cost
was borne by families with incomes below $3,000 under the
administration plan, compared with 8% under the Kennedy-Mills plan.
The administration plan was also more costly for working families with
incomes between $3,000 and $10,000. Such families paid $15 billion
toward the administration plan, compared with $12 billion required
under the Kennedy-Mills plan (p.147). Therefore, the author concluded
that the administration plan was highly regressive over the entire
income range when the costs of the two plans were compared with
income. All these research findings indicate that the single payer plan
is superior to employer mandates in terms of redistributional impacts.

Limitations of Previous Research on NHI: Most existing studies
concentrate on cost estimates rather than the redistributional effects of
national health insurance. Empirical studies which focused on cost
estimates also involve the question of who would bear that cost--

government, employers, or individuals. These studies provide information on the distribution of costs between these three sectors, but few analyze how the proposal have an impact on distribution across income classes.

The Zedlewski et al.(1993) study is the only one that considers the redistributional features of the national health insurance alternatives proposed in the 1980s and 1990s. Although this study presents valuable information, a couple limitations should be addressed. First, Zedlewski et al.(1993) only takes into account the distribution of health care financing across income classes. The distribution of health care benefits across income classes is not considered in their analysis. As discussed by Keintz (1974), under national health insurance incomes can be redistributed through (a) the cost structure in terms of 'who pays how much' and (b) the benefit structure in terms of 'who receives what benefits' (p. 130). In other words, the progressivity of alternative plans is determined by the financing structure of required cost and at the same time by the distribution of medical benefits across income classes. One purpose of national health insurance normally is to redistribute medical resources from the healthy group to the less healthy group rather than from the nonpoor to the poor. However, low-income individuals are likely to have poorer health conditions than those in the middle and upper classes, and thus national health insurance can achieve redistribution through its benefit structure as well. In brief, the redistributional effects may be underestimated in the Zedlewski et al. study. This same problem is found in the Davis (1975) study as well.

Second, all studies have ignored labor supply changes in response to national health insurance. Especially, uniform national health insurance requires increasing taxes for all individuals. At the same time, all individuals would receive benefits in the form of health care services. Effects of increased taxes and benefit receipts on their labor supply behaviors have not been incorporated in any research.

Table 3-3

Prior Cost Estimates For Alternative NHI Program

(dollars in billion)

	Single Payer Plan	Straight Employer Mandate	Play-or-Pay Employer Mandate	Medicaid Expansion	Employer Mandate w/ Medicaid Expansion	Tax Credit
% of uninsured who get coverage	100%	35-75%	100%	35-60%	about 80%	about 100%
Change in nat'l health care spending	-$26 -- +$30	+$10 -- +$15	+$34 -- +$75	+$10 -- +$15	+$12 -- +$20	unclear
Cost to employers	- ?	+$12 -- +$86	+$30 -- +$45	-$5 -- $0	+$8 -- +$26	unchanged
Cost to Government	+ ?	- about $8	+$18 -- +$37	+$26 -- +$33	+$9 -- +$32	-$4 -- +$20
Cost to individuals	unclear	-$5 -- -$14	+$1 -- +$8	-$10 -- -$14	-$8 -- -$22	-$19 -- +$5

Source: EBRI Issue Brief, No. 125, April 1992. (Cited from Lewin (1993), p.10-11).

Why Further Research?

As this literature review of previous proposals and research evidence suggests, anti-poverty reform based on a single program only provides a limited means for resolving the glaring economic conditions for children in the United States. Research evidence indicates that a single proposed program would bring only a small impact: the significant poverty gap and substantial welfare caseloads would still remain. For instance, an assured benefit plan at $3000 would reduce the incidence of poverty only by 20% among custodial parent families even under the most optimistic assumptions (Meyer, Garfinkel, Robins, and Oellerich [1991a]). Eighty percent would still remain in poverty, indicating that child support assurance alone cannot be the remedy for poor children in custodial parent families. Furthermore, child support assurance leaves out many other poor children who do not live in custodial parent families. Even a single program of $1000 children's allowance, which includes all children, can get only 15% of poor children out of poverty (Meyer, Phillips, and Maritato [1991b]). These results from prior research suggest that a more comprehensive reform should be considered. In the search for such a reform, as mentioned in the chapter one, I propose three combined non-income-tested programs-- child support assurance, children's allowance, and national health insurance. No empirical research has been conducted to estimate the effects of these combined programs, although some researchers have assessed the effects of a single program. This study will provide information on what benefits would result at what cost when these programs are combined. The focus of the study is on the interaction effects when programs are combined (compared with a single program), which is different and unavailable from other studies.

At a more specific level, this study seeks to amend the methodological limitations found in previous studies. (Those limitations are discussed earlier.) First, this study will provide a more precise estimate of the gross cost for a child support assurance program. As mentioned earlier, the Current Population Survey (CPS) data on which most previous estimates are based undercounts the number of custodial parents.[16] By using SIPP information from both the child support topical module and household relationship module, this study will correct the undercounted number of custodial parents. This correction will consequently provide a more accurate estimate for the gross cost of the child support assurance system.

Second, all previous studies on child support assurance have not taken into account the benefit package of Medicaid and food stamps which are closely linked to AFDC recipiency. This problem could result in two potential biases: (a) the predicted reductions in AFDC caseloads and expenditures might be overestimated; and (b) estimated net costs might be biased, despite the direction of bias being ambiguous. The biased estimates of net cost are a result of taking overestimated savings on AFDC into a calculation of net cost and not counting the savings from Medicaid and food stamps into net cost. This study will improve this problem by considering the benefits of Medicaid and food stamps in the simulation model. This methodological improvement would bring the same advantages over prior research as for a children's allowance. All existing studies of children's allowance have not considered the possible impact of Medicaid in their simulation models. Meyer, Phillips, and Maritato (1991b) considered food stamps, but ignored Medicaid values, which might have resulted in overstated reduction in AFDC caseloads and AFDC savings. The overestimated AFDC savings again might bias their estimates of net cost.

In brief, this study will have two advantages with respect to costs for child support assurance. The study will (a) capture a more precise gross cost by correcting the undercounted number of custodial parents, and (b) correct some biased direction in net cost estimate by improving the methodological problem of Medicaid and food stamps being closely linked to AFDC. This methodological improvement will also correct overstated effects in prior studies of CSAS or children's allowance on AFDC participation.

Finally, empirical research on the impact of national health insurance on income distribution has been very limited. As addressed before, the prior research has considered only the distribution of financing burden, and ignored the distribution of health care benefits under health care reform. In addition, most reform proposals include a provision for public subsidies to the poor, but no study has estimated the impact on poverty. The prior research on redistribution also has had the methodological limitation of ignoring labor supply changes. By contrast, this study will consider the benefit structure to provide the redistributional features of NHI, which has not been analyzed in prior research. The study will also estimate NHI's effects on poverty along with a discounted rate for health benefits. Finally, this study will incorporate changes in labor supply due to both increased tax rates and universal health care benefits. All together, these will provide a better picture of the impact expected from introduction of national health insurance.

Notes

1. For a graphical presentation of budget sets including AFDC and CSAS, see Meyer, Garfinkel, Robins, & Oellerich (1991), p.10.

2. It should also be considered that the assured benefit of CSAS has an income effect as well--negatively on labor supply. For AFDC custodial parents, however, the guarantee level of CSAS may be higher or lower than that of AFDC depending on the state of residence. If a custodial mother lives in a state whose AFDC guarantee is much lower than the assured level, the CSAS may have an income effect as well as a substitution effect on her labor supply. However if the AFDC guarantee is higher than the assured benefit, the income effect of CSAS does not exist. Thus, the negative income effect of CSAS may be negligible unless the assured benefit of CSAS is set at a substantially high level.

3. Also, see Garfinkel, Manski, & Michalopoulos (1990); Garfinkel (1992).

4. Because he does not present percent changes, these percentages are calculated based on Table 8.7 of Lerman (1989).

5. The plan included a down scale of payments by the order of birth: $420 per year for the first child; $300 for the second, $180 each for the third or the fourth child, $120 for the fifth child, and $60 each for all other children.

6. See Tables 18-20 of Orshansky (1968).

7. The authors simulated two plans for this regard. Under plan A, the increase in income tax liabilities from the repeal of exemptions was limited in such a way that there could be no net loss to a family. Under plan B, exemptions were thoroughly repealed.

8. The authors tested three levels of budget constraint: $3.6, $14.5, and $25 billion, which were net costs after additional tax revenues were counted.

9. For a comparison of demo-grant plan versus NIT, the authors particularly emphasized the percent of cost which goes to close the poverty gap and the amount of 'seepage' of funds to the nonpoor that each scheme allows.

10. See plan d and plan k in Table III (p.150), Musgrave et al.(1970).

11. See Congressional Budget Office (1991); Grumbach et al (1991); U.S. General Accounting Office (1991); Woolhandler and Himmelstein (1991).

12. The Zedlewski et al. simulation employed some assumptions. First, they used different administrative loads for alternative plans: 3% and 5% for the single payer without cost sharing and with cost sharing, respectively; and 7-25% for employer mandates depending on the firm size. Second, the authors considered an increase in health care utilization. Under the single payer plan (without cost sharing), they assume an increase by 11.5% for all individuals; and under all other plans, an increase by 23% for the poor, a linear phase-out for the near-poor, and no change for the nonpoor. Third, the authors assumed that all plans would achieve some savings due to the use of global budgets/expenditure targets, and managed competition. Two levels of cost savings were simulated--4% and 12%.

13. Employer-paid premiums and employer-paid payroll taxes are included in their count of noncash compensation.

14. The administration plan in the 1970s, sponsored by the American Hospital Association, is similar to current employer mandate proposals. The plan consisted of employer-based health insurance for all working families and a federal program replacing Medicaid and Medicare which would cover the elderly, government employees, and all the uninsured.

15. The Kennedy and Mills plan is similar to current single payer proposals. It was a public plan for which 70% of health care expenditures would be financed from tax revenues rather than premiums, and in which a deductible of $150 and a 25% of coinsurance were required.

16. The Lerman (1989) study using the Survey of Incomes and Program Participation (SIPP) might provide a better estimate for a gross cost, if he utilized information on household relationships as well. However, he does not indicate how he figured the custodial status in his analysis. Even assuming that he corrected the undercounting problem, the Lerman study has the methodological drawbacks of ignoring the labor supply effects and AFDC underreporting and of not testing more realistic improvements in private child support. These drawbacks obscure Lerman's further estimates of net cost.

IV

Data And Methods

DATA

The data used is drawn from the 1987 panel of the Survey of Income and Program Participation (SIPP). The panel of 1987 began to interview a nationally representative sample of the civilian noninstitutional population in February 1987. Individuals were interviewed every four months (which is called a 'wave'), and each wave of interviews included information on the previous four months. My main sample is drawn from wave 6 of the 1987 panel, which includes the events of September, 1988. The main reason for choosing wave 6 is that it has a topical module on child support. The sample is defined as a family unit who had children under the age of 18. Using wave 6, total units of families are counted at 4487, including husband/wife families of 3321, female-headed families of 1034, and male-headed families of 132. Because the sample is defined according to an existence of children, some family units which have grandchildren are included in the sample, although there are not many (42 cases).

There are the several advantages of using the SIPP for the purpose of this study. The SIPP was particularly designed to collect detailed information on transfer program recipiency. Questions were asked separately for each transfer program with regard to recipiency and amount of benefits received on a monthly basis. These questions permit identifying a family's participation in AFDC and food stamps, and benefit payments for each month. This monthly information is valuable because most welfare programs are determined on a monthly rather than an annual basis. Moreover, the SIPP provides details of health care coverage including both government programs and private health insurance. These questions include whether there is medical coverage for each person; whether coverage is Medicaid (and/or

Medicare), self-insured, or employer-based; whether coverage is in one's own name or someone else's name; and whether one's plan is the family or individual type. For those covered through employer insurance, questions were further asked about employer contributions to insurance costs. The SIPP also asked about the number of children covered in the household. These SIPP questions allow valuation of health care coverage based on the number of persons covered and the type of health plan. Also, the SIPP contains a special set of questions on child support. The topical module on 'child support agreements' in wave 6 includes questions such as whether a child support agreement exists, what year it was agreed to, what amount of award, how payments were to be made, and what amount received. These questions are important for simulating a child support assurance system (CSAS).

However, the topical module on child support in wave 6 undercounts the number of custodial families. The module asked only for female persons living with children, mainly including divorced mothers of children present from a previous marriage or mothers who indicated receiving child support payments.[1] Thus, the child support module of the SIPP has a similar undercounting problem to that of the CPS: (a) remarried mothers who had children out of wedlock, or who had no children from the most recent divorce but had children from an earlier divorce, are not included unless they marked child support payment; and (b) all custodial fathers are not included. To amend these missing custodial parents potentially eligible for child support, wave 2 is merged into the main sample of wave 6, because wave 2 has a topical module on household relationships. Looking at whether a family has step children, those potential custodial parents are determined and matched to the sample. This mergence brings the total number of custodial families to 1441: 925 single-mother families; 131 single-father families; 318 two-parent families in which mothers had children from absent fathers; 40 two-parent families in which fathers had children from absent mothers; and 27 two-parent families in which both mother and father had child-support related children. In the mergence of wave 2 with the main sample of wave 6, some missing cases (149) result because of different points of time. Those cases of wave 2 not matched to the main sample must be eliminated, although they truncate the number of custodial families. However, the merged data is expected to correct some undercounting of custodial families.

Another problem of wave 6 is that it does not have information on shelter costs, which is needed to impute food stamps. To get this information, wave 7 is also merged into the main sample, which provides amounts of rent and utilities paid during the survey month. In this mergence, some missing cases again result, but the sample mean of shelter cost has been assigned for these missing cases.

METHODS

The simulation of proposed program(s) involves several intermediate steps which include figuring incomes and taxes under the current situation, setting up policy changes under the post reform, and predicting behavior responses to welfare participation and labor supply due to the implementation of proposed program(s). The current situation in the simulation is defined as all incomes and taxes that a family received or paid out as of the year 1988. Current income sources include earnings, private child support, EITC, AFDC benefit, cash values of food stamps and health insurance coverage such as Medicaid and employer-based insurance, and all other taxable or nontaxable incomes. Taxes counted in simulation include income and payroll taxes that the family paid out during the same period of time. The net income is then defined as the gross income minus income and payroll taxes.

For the purpose of simulation, it is necessary to estimate or impute some of the income sources and taxes, because the SIPP lacks the information or because reported information has an underreporting problem. This section describes how each source of incomes and taxes has been determined under the current economic situation. Also, it describes how income sources and taxes change under the post reform, and how these changes affect an individual's behaviors in terms of program participation and labor supply decisions.

AFDC and Food Stamp Imputation

AFDC Imputation: Because of underreporting problems, one of the intermediate steps is to estimate the amount of AFDC received. For instance, Marquis and Moore (1989) indicated that the SIPP respondents reported 37% lower participation. From my sample, reported AFDC cases account for only 70% of what it should be based on administrative records.[2] To correct this underreporting, the amount of AFDC reported is ignored, but each family's income eligibility for AFDC is first calculated. To determine if a family is income eligible for AFDC, I utilize the maximum amount of AFDC available for the family based on the state of residence and family size, and the tax rate on earnings estimated by Fraker, Moffitt and Wolfe (1985). If a family is income eligible, an AFDC benefit is then computed for the family according to what the formula would say.[3] This procedure brings up three types of cases in AFDC imputation: (a) cases which reported recipiency and were income-eligible; (b) cases which did not report but were income-eligible; and (c) cases which reported but were income-ineligible for AFDC. The cases in the first category are all assigned to AFDC cases. The second category of cases may represent underreported recipiency. However, a simple check of income eligibility in this type of cases can result in overestimated recipiency for two reasons. First, two-parent families are not likely to receive AFDC benefits even though they are income-eligible. On the other hand, mother-only families are more likely to receive benefits if they are income-eligible. Therefore, among cases which did not report but were income-eligible, only mother-only families are assigned as AFDC recipients. Second, another source of overestimation is related to cases whose levels of income are slightly below the eligibility standard. These cases are income-eligible, but their amounts of benefit are rather small and perhaps they may not be real AFDC recipients. So single-mother families who are income-eligible but whose benefits are calculated less than $1000 are further screened and treated as non-AFDC cases. Finally, the third category of cases (reported but income-ineligible) is problematic; they probably are associated with misreporting. These problem cases are assigned as AFDC recipients, but constrained not to change program participation and labor supply, because these cases cause a problem for labor supply simulation. Labor supply simulation involves checking income-eligibility under each point of hours worked under the post reform. When a change in hours of work is allowed, the case is very likely moving off AFDC because it is currently income-ineligible. This could result in overestimating the reduction in AFDC caseloads. For this reason, the third type of AFDC cases are constrained not to change labor supply under the reform.

In all AFDC cases assigned in this way, reported amounts of AFDC benefit are ignored, but estimated amounts of AFDC from the formula are employed, since consistency should be maintained between pre and post treatments of AFDC benefits. For example, when new transfers such as assured benefits and children allowances are introduced, AFDC benefit amounts will change accordingly. Changes in AFDC benefit under the post reform can be figured only by the AFDC formula. As long as amounts of AFDC benefit for the post reform have to be calculated according to the formula, the use of reported amounts of AFDC for the current situation could cause an inconsistency in determining benefits. For this reason, calculated amounts of AFDC based on the formula are employed instead of reported amounts.

This AFDC imputation procedure results in total caseloads of 3.8 million and total benefit payments of $16 billion with a mean AFDC benefit of $4215. Since child support collections are estimated at about $1.8 billion for AFDC cases, the net public cost of AFDC benefits is $15.1 billion. These estimated totals are very close to the public AFDC statistics as of 1988.[4] Among the 3.8 million AFDC cases, 58% account for cases reported as well as income-eligible; 31% for cases income-eligible but not reported; and 11% for cases reported but income-ineligible. All AFDC families account for 10.4% of total families with children under age 18.

Food Stamp Imputation: In the same way as for AFDC imputation, income eligibility of each family for food stamps is first examined. Several steps are used to check whether or not a family is eligible for the program. First, a family's gross monthly income is defined as the sum of earnings, AFDC benefit, child support, and all other income. Second, a counted monthly income (say, CMI_a) is computed by subtracting certain deductions from the gross monthly income. The deductions include an inflation-indexed standard deduction ($106), taxes and work expenses (20% of any earned income), and out-of-pocket dependent care expenses up to $160 for each dependent. Third, the counted monthly income (CMI_a) is further adjusted for shelter expenses exceeding 50% of CMI_a and the ceiling set at $170 (say, CMI_b).[5] Finally, an amount of food stamps benefit is calculated from the maximum allotment (established by family size) minus 30% of CMI_b.[6] If a family is computed to have a positive amount of benefits, the family is considered income-eligible for food stamps. However, only checking income eligibility could result in an overstated number of families receiving food stamps. It has been reported that a substantial number of eligible households did not get food stamps because of stigma or inconvenience. Therefore, cases are further screened according to the following criteria. First, income-eligible cases who reported recipiency are assigned as recipients. Second, AFDC cases including imputed cases are assigned as food stamp recipients if they report food stamps.[7] Once a family is defined as a food stamp recipient from these steps, the cash value of food stamps computed by the formula is used for the benefit amount received (and reported amounts of food stamps are ignored).

From food stamp imputation, about 3.6 million families are estimated to receive food stamps of $2049 on average, and spend total benefit payments of $7.3 billion as of 1988.[8] These food stamp families account for 9.7% of all families with children under the age of 18.

Estimating Gross Wage Rates

Simulation of labor supply requires a variable of net wage rate. To obtain a net wage per hour, a gross wage should first be defined. To do this, the following procedure is used separately for workers and nonworkers. For workers, reported information in the data is basically utilized, but for nonworkers a gross-wage equation is estimated to impute their hourly wage rates. This intermediate step is to prepare for the simulation model allowing labor supply changes in nonworkers as well as workers responding to reform program(s).

Gross Wages for Workers: The SIPP asked about hourly wage rates only for persons with hourly-paid jobs. The reported hourly wages for this group of people are primarily utilized. For individuals with non-hourly-paid jobs, however, wage rates need to be derived based on other available information in the data. For this purpose, three sources of information are utilized from the SIPP. First, the SIPP provides the number of weeks worked for each job for the employed and self-employed (up to two jobs each) during the survey month. Second, the SIPP further provides the number of hours worked per week in those jobs during the month. Using these two sources of information, the total number of hours worked in all jobs during the month is calculated.[9] Third, the SIPP has monthly amounts of earnings from each employed job 1 and job 2. In addition, amounts of earnings from self-employed job 1 and job 2 are separately collected during the month. The total amount of earnings from all jobs during the month is obtained by adding up all these sources of earnings. Finally to produce an hourly gross wage for a person with non-hourly-paid job(s), this total amount of earnings is divided by the total number of hours worked during the month.

Gross Wages for Nonworkers: Hourly gross wages need to be imputed for current nonworkers, because the data provides no job-related information for these individuals. For this purpose, a log gross wage equation is estimated separately from four subgroups of current workers: black males, nonblack males, black females, and nonblack females. However, the use of equation estimated from a working population in order to impute wages of nonworkers carries a sample selection bias (i.e., upward bias). There is a difference in certain characteristics between nonworkers and workers. To correct this selection bias, a two-stage estimation procedure is employed.

As the first step, a probit selection equation is estimated according to the following model:

$$E(LS^*) = F(\alpha * S) \quad ..... \quad (Eqt \ 4\text{-}1)$$

where LS^* is a latent variable and LS is the observed variable for earnings ($LS = 1$ if $LS^* > 0$, $= 0$ otherwise); $S =$ vector of demographic attributes; and $\alpha =$ vector of coefficients. This probit equation is estimated separately for black mothers, nonblack mothers, black fathers, and nonblack fathers, all including nonworkers as well as workers.

As the second stage, then, the log-wage equation is estimated based on ordinary least squares:

$$E(log(W)) = \Sigma(\beta_1 * T + \beta_2 * LAMBDA) \quad ..... \quad (Eqt \ 4\text{-}2)$$

where $log(W) =$ log term of gross wage per hour; $T =$ vector of demographic attributes; $LAMBDA =$ selection-bias term; and β's $=$

vector of coefficients. As in the first stage, the log-wage equation is estimated separately for the four groups by sex (female and male) and race (black and nonblack), but including only workers. Explanatory variables in these equations--such as region, unemployment rate of state, metropolitan area, age, age square, education levels, interaction term of education and age, marital status, health condition, other income sources, and children-related variables--are included.

Tables 4-1 and 4-2 present estimated equations of gross wage separately from mothers and fathers. Table 4-1(A) shows equation estimates of mothers' work participation from the sample of all nonblack mothers (3645) and of black mothers (524), separately. Table 4-1(B) includes wage equations estimated from working mothers. Since nonworking mothers are excluded in these equations, the size of samples employed is reduced to 2061 for nonblack mothers and 278 for black mothers. As seen in Table 4-1 (A & B), some variables are statistically significant for explaining their labor participation and wage rates. As expected, age and education levels are positively related to a mother's work and wage. Also, marital status is particularly associated with a mother's work decision. For nonblack as well as black mothers, the state rate of unemployment is predicted to have a negative effect on a mother's work attendance and wage. A mother's health condition and child-related variables are other significant predictors. These results generally confirm to human capital theory. However, as Table 4-1(B) demonstrates, a parameter of selection bias (LAMBDA) is not significant for either nonblack or black mothers. This means that the error term from the first state regression is not related to the error term of the log-wage function for mothers. In other words, there is no selection bias in the results of log-wage function for mothers.

For fathers, Table 4-2 (A & B) presents estimated equations for labor participation and wages. Particularly for father's participation in labor force, as Table 4-2(A) indicates, only a few variables are significant as explanatory variables, including age, health condition, and other income. This especially contrasts with the nonblack mothers participation equation in which many explanatory variables were significant (see Table 4-1(A)). This different pattern appears to demonstrate that a mother's participation in the labor force is more dependent on her individual characteristics, while a father's is more dependent on social factors (e.g., social norm) other than his own. Given participation, however, similar variables explain a father's wage at a significant level, as predicted by human capital theory. These variables include age, education, region, metropolitan area, and health status.

Some different patterns are found in labor participation and wages between black and nonblack fathers. First, as seen in Table 4-2(A), marital status is a significant variable for a black father's labor participation, but insignificant for a nonblack father's. Given work participation, as Table 4-2(B) shows, a second interesting contrast in the variable of unemployment rate: a black father's wage is negatively affected by the unemployment rate of his residing state, while that variable is insignificant for a nonblack father's wage. Another difference between these two groups is found in LAMBDA, which represents a selection bias. Table 4-2 (B) shows a significant coefficient of LAMBDA for black fathers, but an insignificant one for nonblack fathers.

These estimated equations are used to impute the hourly gross wage of nonworkers. By using estimated coefficients, a wage is predicted given each nonworker's characteristics.[10] Since the dependent variable of the wage equation is expressed as a log term, the predicted log-wage is converted into the regular term of hourly wage by using standard errors of regression.[11] The mean of predicted wage rate for nonworkers is $8.9 for nonblack mothers; $6 for black mothers; $13.5 for nonblack fathers; and $7.7 for black fathers.

Table 4-1
Equation Estimates Of Gross Wages For Mothers

1. Participation Equation
   (Maximum Likelihood Probit Estimates)

Dependent Variable=1 if Positive Amount of Employment Earnings, =0 Otherwise

	Nonblack Mothers(N=3645)		Black Mothers(N=524)	
constant	-0.8739	(-2.16)**	-0.7009	(-0.74)
age	0.0744	(3.90)***	0.0780	(1.76)*
age square	-0.0010	(-4.69)***	-0.0011	(-2.37)**
9 < = educ <12	0.1253	(0.84)	-0.0423	(-0.11)
educ= 12	0.4346	(2.63)***	0.4461	(1.00)
12< educ <16	0.6077	(3.07)***	0.6366	(1.18)
educ > = 16	0.7377	(2.93)***	1.0712	(1.52)
educ*ag	-0.0000	(-0.05)	0.0007	(0.39)
divorced/widowed	0.5207	(6.76)***	0.1507	(0.82)
separated	0.2285	(1.90)*	0.1513	(0.72)
never married	-0.0654	(-0.56)	-0.3941	(-2.43)**
unemployment rate	-0.0777	(-4.37)***	-0.1015	(-2.54)**
south	0.2370	(3.58)***	0.0921	(0.32)
midwest	0.1895	(2.98)***	-0.0332	(-0.11)
north east	-0.1304	(-1.79)*	-0.2595	(-0.86)
city	-0.0222	(-0.32)	0.1876	(0.87)
smsa	0.0342	(0.53)	-0.2662	(-1.41)
health	-0.7228	(-8.72)***	-1.1382	(-4.82)***
other income	-0.0003	(-2.94)***	-0.0006	(-1.37)
preschool chdrn	-0.4080	(-6.86)***	-0.2968	(-1.90)*
no. of chdrn > =3	-0.2173	(-3.77)***	-0.0991	(-0.67)
Log-Likelihood	-2271.5		-294.9	
Mean Percentage (with Earnings)	56.6		53.1	

Data Source: 1987 Panel of SIPP Wave 6

T-statistics in parentheses:
*** significant at less than 1% level;
** significant at 1-5% level;
* significant at 5-10% level.

Table 4-1 continues.

2. Gross Wage Rate Equation

Dependent Variable= Log of Hourly Wage

	Nonblack Mothers(N=2061)		Black Mothers(N=278)	
constant	0.3928	(1.27)	0.5287	(0.67)
age	0.0766	(5.96)***	0.0704	(2.06)**
age square	-0.0011	(-7.01)***	-0.0009	(-2.13)**
9 < = educ <12	-0.0750	(-0.80)	-0.0821	(-0.42)
educ=12	-0.0416	(-0.39)	0.1380	(0.53)
12 < educ< 16	0.0825	(0.66)	0.3377	(1.05)
educ >=16	0.2574	(1.64)*	0.7050	(1.66)*
educ*age	0.0008	(2.56)***	0.0004	(0.43)
divorced/widowed	0.0470	(1.08)	0.1167	(1.42)
separated	-0.0363	(-0.57)	0.1089	(1.17)
never married	0.0566	(0.80)	-0.0983	(-0.98)
unemployment rate	-0.0368	(-3.56)***	-0.0614	(-2.32)**
south	0.0201	(0.53)	-0.1730	(-1.35)
midwest	-0.0384	(-1.07)	-0.0734	(-0.58)
north east	-0.0352	(-0.88)	-0.1389	(-1.01)
city	0.1088	(2.94)***	0.0220	(0.23)
smsa	0.1287	(3.80)***	-0.0261	(-0.30)
health	-0.1176	(-1.62)*	-0.5178	(-2.00)**
LAMBDA	0.0601	(0.56)	0.3596	(1.12)

R - Squared	0.20		0.27
Mean of Logwage	2.07		1.95
Standard Error	0.52		0.50
(Corrected for Selection)			

Data Source: 1987 Panel of SIPP Wave 6

Notes:
  (a) educ= years of education
  (b) unemployment rate= the rate of female unemployment in her state of residence;
  (c) health= 1 if disabled, has poor health or health conditions limiting the amount or kind of work;
  (d) other income= the sum of asset income, other taxable income, and child support payments received;
  (e) preschool chdrn= 1 if she has preschool child(ren);
  (f) no. of chdrn >=3 is one if the number of children is equal to or greater than three.

Table 4-2
Equation Estimates Of Gross Wages For Fathers

1. Participation Equation
   (Maximum Likelihood Probit Estimates)

Dependent Variable= 1 if Positive Amount of Employment Earnings, = 0 Otherwise

	Nonblack Fathers(N=2745)		Black Fathers(N=237)	
constant	-0.6644	(-1.18)	0.6549	(0.28)
age	0.1090	(4.31)***	0.1108	(1.13)
age square	-0.0016	(-5.83)***	-0.0021	(-2.18)**
9 < = educ <12	0.0550	(0.28)	-1.3671	(-1.25)
educ= 12	0.2057	(0.92)	-1.1484	(-0.89)
12< educ <16	0.1674	(0.62)	-0.2118	(-0.13)
educ >= 16	0.4396	(1.26)	0.4779	(0.21)
educ*age	0.0006	(0.92)	0.0029	(0.75)
divorced/widowed	-0.2488	(-1.28)	2.8576	(0.01)
separated	-0.1626	(-0.44)	-3.0643	(-2.55)***
never married	-0.4622	(-0.89)	-1.2960	(-1.90)*
unemployment rate	0.0176	(0.77)	-0.0050	(-1.05)
south	-0.0798	(-0.76)	0.5813	(0.84)
midwest	-0.0619	(-0.56)	0.6932	(0.98)
north east	0.1201	(0.93)	0.2394	(0.32)
city	0.0328	(0.28)	-0.7110	(-1.26)
smsa	0.0963	(0.86)	-0.2598	(-0.61)
health	-0.8989	(-9.25)***	-2.3068	(-5.38)***
other income	-0.0006	(-5.40)***	-0.0026	(-3.44)***
no. of chdrn >=3	-0.2285	(-2.49)**	0.2168	(0.61)
Log-Likelihood	-692.6		-51.3	
Mean Percentage (with Earnings)	87.8		77.2	

Data Source: 1987 Panel of SIPP Wave 6

T-statistics in parentheses:
*** significant at less than 1% level;
** significant at 1-5% level;
* significant at 5-10% level.

Table 4-2 continues.

2. Gross Wage Rate Equation

Dependent Variable= Log of Hourly Wage

	Nonblack Fathers(N=2407)		Black Fathers(N=183)	
constant	0.6180	(2.72)***	1.3589	(2.86)***
age	0.0645	(6.21)***	0.0407	(1.81)*
age square	-0.0008	(-5.70)***	-0.0006	(-2.29)**
9 < = educ <12	0.0110	(0.18)	0.0790	(0.41)
educ=12	0.1664	(2.38)**	0.0539	(0.24)
12 < educ< 16	0.2337	(2.81)***	0.2403	(0.91)
educ >=16	0.3787	(3.57)***	0.3152	(0.91)
educ*age	0.0006	(2.92)***	0.0007	(0.96)
divorced/widowed	-0.0314	(-0.53)	0.1759	(0.55)
separated	-0.1926	(-1.79)*	-0.3277	(-1.31)
never married	-0.2372	(-1.43)	-0.1346	(-0.74)
unemployment rate	-0.0042	(-0.68)	-0.0544	(-3.14)***
south	-0.0930	(-3.50)***	-0.0184	(-0.12)
midwest	0.0073	(0.27)	0.2107	(1.31)
north east	0.0707	(2.26)**	0.0834	(0.50)
city	0.1091	(3.56)***	-0.0452	(-0.47)
smsa	0.0847	(3.00)***	0.0258	(0.31)
health	-0.2637	(-3.97)***	-0.3590	(-2.38)**
LAMBDA	0.1575	(0.93)	0.3891	(2.91)***
R - Squared	0.28		0.28	
Mean of Logwage	2.49		2.22	
Standard Error	0.46		0.41	
(Corrected for Selection)				

Data Source: 1987 Panel of SIPP Wave 6

Notes:

  (a) educ= years of education

  (b) unemployment rate= the rate of female unemployment in his state of residence;

  (c) health= 1 if disabled, has poor health or health conditions limiting the amount or kind of work;

  (d) other income= the sum of asset income, other taxable income, and child support payments received;

  (e) no. of chdrn >=3 is one if the number of children is equal to or greater than three.

Figuring Current Tax System

The SIPP did not ask about taxes paid out or earned income tax credits (EITC) claimed. Therefore, both income and payroll taxes[12] and EITC are calculated on the basis of income information for each family. Since an annual figure of income is needed to calculate income taxes and EITC, annual income is obtained by multiplying monthly income by 12.

Earned Income Tax Credits: For the fiscal year 1988, EITC eligibility requires that (a) annual earned income is not zero and (b) gross taxable income unadjusted for standard deduction and personal exemptions is less than $18,576. Up to $6,224, the credit is 14% of earned income. The maximum credit of $874 is reached between incomes of $6,225 and $9,850. This maximum credit is then reduced by 10 cents for each dollar of gross taxable income (or, if greater, earned income) in excess of $9,850. Consequently, EITC is phased out for tax payers with gross taxable income (or, if greater, earned income) above $18,576. These counts result in total EITC at $4.4 billion, and the mean of credits claimed at $520 for families eligible for EITC.[13]

Income Taxes: To figure the amount of income taxes that each family paid during 1988, a somewhat simplified model of the tax system is established: all married couples are assumed to file jointly, and all single parents are assumed to file as a head of household; and deductions other than the standard deduction are ignored since data on itemization is not available. Tax liability is calculated on the basis of the taxable income[14] minus the standard deduction and an exemption for each individual in the family. In 1988, the standard deduction was $5,000 for joint filing status and $3,000 for single filing status. The personal exemption was $1,950. Once the adjusted gross income for the deduction and exemptions is established, an amount of income tax liability is computed by using the tax rate of the tax bracket to which a family belongs.[15] This procedure results in the total amount of income taxes at $139 billion, and the mean amount of income taxes at $4613 for families with a positive tax liability. This estimate is in a reasonable range. The U.S. Bureau of Census (1990, November) reports $4415 as of 1988 for the average amount of income taxes which were collected from 31 million households with related children under age 18. These figures reveal a total income tax of $137.4 billion. Thus, my estimate of $139 billion is overestimated by $1.6 billion, probably due to ignoring itemized deductions in income tax calculations.

Payroll Taxes: A payroll tax is imposed on earnings up to a specific dollar amount. All persons who work in covered employment are required to pay the mandatory tax on their earnings and employers pay an equal tax rate for these workers. As of 1988, the tax paid by each of employer and employee was 7.51% of the first $45,000 of earnings. Since the extracted data does not include whether one's employed job is covered or not, it is assumed that all persons with employed jobs paid 7.51% of their earnings up to the maximum amount of $45,000. All self-employed workers also are required to pay payroll taxes that are equivalent to the combined employer-employee rate. However, the tax system as of 1988 gave self-employment credits, which on average accounted for 2% of self-employment incomes.[16] Subtracting 2% from the combined tax rate (15.02%), 13.02% of self-employed earnings up to $45,000 is taxed as a payroll tax. As a result, total payroll taxes are estimated at $81.8 billion; the mean of payroll taxes paid is $2549 for those with earnings.

Changes in Child Support Situation

Assumptions for Improvement in Private Child Support: The variable of child support payment is critical for simulation of the child support assurance system (CSAS). In general, amounts of private child support received are expected to increase under CSAS. As mentioned earlier, the proposed CSAS has the automatic income withholding provision as well as the incentive component requiring that cases must have awards to receive the assured benefit. As a result of these provisions, CSAS is expected to improve both percentages of collection and incidence of award. However, we currently lack a reliable estimate on the extent of improvement in child support under the assurance system. Thus, some assumptions are carried out for plausible changes in post child support dimensions.

The amount of child support depends on the incidence of award, the level of that award, and the percentage of the award collected. Either or all of these three dimensions of child support can be improved to secure certain levels of child support. The most pessimistic view would assume that current incidence and levels of award and current percentages of collection would continue with no improvement. On the other hand, the most optimistic view would assume that all custodial parents will secure awards with a nationally standardized level and collect full payments owed (perfect system). In this study, two scenarios will be simulated for the post private child support situation. First, this study will simulate the worst case by using current child support payments, assuming no change in any of the child support dimensions. This scenario is to provide the most conservative estimate for CSAS. The second scenario assumes a medium improvement in private child support. The medium improvement means that award levels are established by the percentage standard formula, and rates of award and collection increase by half the distance from the current to the perfect system. This second scenario is to provide a more realistic picture of the CSAS performance.

Estimating Private Child Support Variables: Amounts of private child support received are a basic variable for simulation of CSAS. The SIPP data reported amounts of private child support received by custodial mothers during the year. However, the reported information is ignored, and estimation procedures are instead employed in this study. A primary reason for this is to allow increases in award incidence and child support collection under the medium improvement scenario in child support. Since the amount of private child support depends on some different dimensions of child support, three equations are estimated: (a) the probability of having award, (b) the collection rate, and (c) the amount of child support payment.

First, for the probability of award, a logit equation is estimated according to:

$$E(log[P_{aw}/(1-P_{aw})]) = \Sigma(\delta * X) \ ..... \ (Eqt \ 4\text{-}3)$$

where $log(P_{aw})$ = log term of probability of having an award; $X=$ vector of demographic attributes; and $\delta=$ vector of coefficients. The vector of independent variables includes the absent father's income (estimated), dummies of race, marital status, and region, the number of children present from the absent father, and the presence of preschool child(ren). The estimated logit equation from all custodial mothers (n= 1284) is presented in Table 4-3. The coefficients indicate that the more the absent father earns, the more a custodial mother is likely to obtain an award; that hispanics and blacks are less likely to have awards than whites; that compared to a remarried mother, a divorced mother is more likely to have an award but a separated or never-marred mother is less likely to have an award; and finally that the more children are present, the greater likelihood of having an award. These patterns are similar to those observed in previous research.[17]

With the estimated logit, the probability of having an award for each custodial parent eligible for private child support is then computed by:

$$P_{aw} = exp[E(AW)] / [1 + exp[E(AW)] \quad ..... \quad (Eqt\ 4\text{-}4)$$

where $E(AW)$ is the expected value obtained based on Eqt 4-3. From Eqt 4-4, the predicted probability of each case falls in the range of 0 and 1, whose fraction (i.e., P_{aw}) represents some families in the universe with a child support award; and the rest of fraction of that case (i.e., $1 - P_{aw}$) represents those families with no award. Therefore, if we multiply the sample weight by the predicted probability of having an award for each family and add up these multiplied outcomes, the resulting sum then represents the total number of families with awards in the population. The current rate of award, then, can be obtained with the total number of families with awards divided by the total families eligible for child support. This current rate of award in the population will serve as the baseline for an improvement in award incidence. The medium improvement involves an increase of the current award rate by half the distance to the perfect establishment of award in the aggregate level. To reach this under the medium improvement scenario, the probability of award predicted for each custodial parent (i.e., P_{aw}) is increased by half.

Second, even after a family has secured an award, its payment is still subject to uncertainty. The absent parent may pay the full amount originally awarded, less than the original level, or nothing. Thus, post improvement in child support can be achieved by increasing the current percentage of collection. For this purpose, regression equation for current collection rates given awards is estimated according to an ordinary least squares procedure. The regression equation is modelled as:

$$E(CR) = \Sigma(\gamma * Y) \ \ldots.. \ (Eqt \ 4-5)$$

where CR = collection rate, which is defined as the amount of child support received divided by the amount of award; Y = vector of demographic attributes; and γ = vector of coefficients. As explanatory variables, almost the same set of independent variables (as those for the probability of award) are employed, except the number of eligible children. Since the category of custodial mothers with no awards is not relevant for collection, the sample size available for estimation (custodial mothers with awards) is reduced to 659. Table 4-4 presents estimated coefficients from this reduced sample. The estimated income variable of the absent father shows a strongly positive relation with the collection rate. The race coefficients are negative, but not significantly different from zero (except black), probably because of the smaller sample size. It is also indicated that those living in the west are likely to be paid smaller amounts than those in the north central area. It is of interest to note that never-married custodial parents are likely to receive a higher percentage of the child support owed. This fact is perhaps due to selectivity. Most never-married mothers do not have awards; those with awards are likely to have different characteristics than the married population in general. Another possible explanation is that never-married parents are more likely to make contact with a Child Support Enforcement agency to secure awards and make collections through the agency's supports.

With the estimated equation, the predicted rate of collection for each custodial parent serves as the baseline for an improvement in collection rate under the post reform. To achieve the aggregate collection of half the distance from the current to the perfect collection, the predicted rate of collection for each individual is increased by half.

Finally, the amount of child support received given an award is estimated by an ordinary least squares technique as follows:

$$E(CS) = \Sigma(\sigma * Z) \ \ldots.. \ (Eqt \ 4-6)$$

where CS = amount of child support received; Z = vector of demographic attributes; and σ = vector of coefficients. The similar set of explanatory variables is employed for this equation, including the absent father's income, race, marital status, region, and the number of eligible child(ren). Table 4-5 presents the coefficients estimated from

659 custodial mothers with awards. The variable of absent father's income indicates an increase of $108 in child support payment per thousand of absent father's income. Also indicated is that divorced, separated, and never-married mothers are likely to collect more payments than a remarried mother does on average: $762 more for the divorced, $695 more for the separated, and $1000 for the never-married. These all imply that once the mother has married, the absent father is not likely to continue the original payments. The higher level of payment predicted for a never-married mother again appears related to public child support enforcement. As another significant variable, the estimated equation indicates an increase in payment by $375 per child present of the absent father. By using this estimated equation, an amount of current child support is predicted for each custodial parent based on her characteristics.

It should be noted that having awards does not always mean receiving child support payments. Some mothers awarded receive nothing. Since these mothers (awarded but not paid) are included for estimation of collection rate and child support payment, means of predicted collection rate and payment can be lower than those among mothers paid.

As addressed in the data section, SIPP wave 6 asked only mothers living with children about child support, missing custodial fathers. These three equations, therefore, are estimated from mothers who were living with children from absent fathers. However, the sample includes fathers living with children from their absent mother, whose custodial status was figured based on household relationships (wave 2) rather than the child support module. Since these custodial fathers do not have child support information, they need to be imputed an award probability, collection rate, and child support paid. For this, since we lack nationally representative information, I adopt information on custodial fathers based on the Wisconsin data which collected court records of child support. In the state of Wisconsin as of 1985, the percentage of custodial fathers with awards was 27%; collection rate on average was 44%; and the mean amount of child support awarded was $2,067 among those with awards. For custodial fathers in the sample, these means are used for the probability of award, collection rate, and amount of child support received (i.e., 2067*.44).

The three child support equations listed above all include the absent father's income as an independent variable in their equation models. In addition, the use of the percentage standard formula for establishing award levels under the medium improvement requires information on the absent father's income. Since the SIPP data does not report the incomes of noncustodial parents, estimating procedures developed by Oellerich (1984) are employed to impute the absent father's income.[18]

Table 4-3
Equation Estimates Of Probability Of Having Award
(Maximum Likelihood Logit Estimates)

Dependent Variable= 1 if a positive amount of child support was due in 1988, = 0 otherwise

constant	-0.6448	(-2.09) **
absent father's income	0.0354	(3.50) ***
hispanic	-1.0124	(-4.34) ***
black	-0.5781	(-3.33) ***
divorced	0.5940	(3.86) ***
separated	-0.3563	(-1.84) *
never-married	-1.0071	(-4.75) ***
north east	-0.2060	(-1.09)
south	-0.0764	(-0.47)
west	0.0790	(0.43)
no. of chdrn eligible	0.1685	(2.52) ***
presence of preschool chdrn	0.1676	(1.21)

Log-Likelihood   -772.2
Percentage with Awards   51
N= 1284 (custodial mothers living with
        children of the absent father)

Data Source: 1987 Panel of SIPP Wave 6

Notes:
  (a) Absent father's income is predicted according to the equation estimates by Garfinkel and Oellerich (1989), and descaled by dividing by 1,000;
  (b) 'Black' refers to non-hispanic blacks and the omitted dummy of race refers to non-hispanic whites and non-hispanic others;
  (c) T-statistics in parentheses:
      *** significant at less than 1% level;
      ** significant at 1-5% level;
      * significant at 5-10% level.

Table 4-4
Equation Estimates Of Collection Rate
(Ordinary Least Squares Estimates)

Dependent Variable= child support received divided by child support due in 1988

constant	0.4456	(5.86) ***
absent father's income	0.0096	(3.67) ***
hispanic	-0.1015	(-1.36)
black	-0.0924	(-1.73) *
divorced	0.0429	(1.14)
separated	0.0187	(0.34)
never-married	0.1452	(2.08) **
north east	0.0299	(0.59)
south	0.0160	(0.38)
west	-0.0994	(-2.14) **
presence of preschool chdrn	0.0178	(0.48)

R-Squared	0.05
Mean of Collection Rate	0.66

N= 659 (custodial mothers with awards)

Data Source: 1987 Panel of SIPP Wave 6

Notes:
  (a) Absent father's income is predicted according to the equation estimates by Garfinkel and Oellerich (1989), and descaled by dividing by 1,000;
  (b) 'Black' refers to non-hispanic blacks and the omitted dummy of race refers to non-hispanic whites and non-hispanic others;
  (c) T-statistics in parentheses:
     *** significant at less than 1% level;
     ** significant at 1-5% level;
     * significant at 5-10% level.

Table 4-5
Equation Estimates Of Amount Of Child Support Received
(Ordinary Least Squares Estimates)

Dependent Variable= child support received in 1988

constant	-1180.34	(-2.75) ***
absent father's income	108.30	(7.53) ***
hispanic	-714.18	(-1.62) *
black	-338.67	(-1.08)
divorced	761.72	(3.48) ***
separated	694.84	(2.13) **
never-married	999.88	(2.47) ***
north east	96.75	(0.32)
south	-241.17	(-0.97)
west	-469.70	(-1.73) *
no. of chdrn eligible	374.91	(3.33) ***

R-Squared	0.13
Mean Amount Received	$2,021

N= 659 (custodial mothers with awards)

Data Source: 1987 Panel of SIPP Wave 6

Notes:
  (a) Absent father's income is predicted according to the equation estimates by Garfinkel and Oellerich (1989), and descaled by dividing by 1,000;
  (b) 'Black' refers to non-hispanic blacks and the omitted dummy of race refers to non-hispanic whites and non-hispanic others;
  (c) T-statistics in parentheses:
    *** significant at less than 1% level;
    ** significant at 1-5% level;
    * significant at 5-10% level.

Reported and Simulated Private Child Support: From the SIPP as of September 1988, the number of all custodial parents living with children under age 18 who are eligible for private child support is estimated at 12.1 million. Among these, custodial mothers are 10.7 million, and custodial fathers are 1.4 million. As expected, the total number of custodial mothers is larger than that estimated from the Current Population Survey (CPS). Based on the CPS data, 9.4 million was the reported number of women with own children under 21 years of age who were present from absent fathers as of Spring 1988 (U.S. Bureau of Census, 1990 (June, Table B). Although the CPS data additionally include those living with children aged between 18 and 20, the number of custodial mothers is undercounted by 1.3 million, compared to the SIPP data. As discussed earlier, this difference results because the CPS data missed mothers who had no children from the most recent divorce or separation, but had children from an earlier divorce or separation; and it is also because the CPS data did not count mothers who are currently married but had children out of wedlock. On the other hand, my estimate corrects those undercounts by using information on household relationships available in SIPP.

    Based on the estimated equations listed above, Table 4-6 presents the simulated variables and their aggregate totals with respect to private child support. From the simulated child support variables under the current situation (the first panel in Table 4-6), 48% of all custodial parents (including custodial fathers) have awards whose amounts awarded are aggregated to $17 billion in 1988 dollars. The estimated total of child support collected is $11.4 billion, indicating an aggregate collection rate of 67%. The mean of child support currently collected is estimated at $2041 for mothers, $1002 for fathers and $1973 for all custodial parents. The second panel of Table 4-6 presents aggregate totals under the assumption of medium improvement in child support. The post award rate of all parents increases to 74% by improving award establishments by half; award levels based on the Wisconsin percentage standard increase to $40.8 billion in total; and a half-way increase in collection rate raises the total collection to $30.3 billion (74% implied for aggregate collection rate), which averages $3388 for all custodial parents awarded.

Table 4-6
Private Child Support Variables

(All Dollar Amounts in 1988)

	Mothers	Fathers	All Parents
Current Child Support Situation			
Absent Parent's Mean Income	$10,700	$21,735	$20,474
No. of Custodial Families	(million) 10.7	(million) 1.4	(million) 12.1
Award Rate: Reported Simulated	51% 50.3%	n.a 27.3%	n.a 48%
Total Amt Awarded: Reported Simulated	(billion) $15.9 $16.1	(billion) n.a $0.86	(billion) n.a $17.0
Total Amt Collected: Reported Simulated	(billion) $11.0 $11.0	(billion) n.a $0.38	(billion) n.a $11.4
Collection Rate: Reported Simulated	69% 68.3%	n.a 44%	n.a 67%
Mean Amt Collected: * Reported Simulated	$1,989 $2,041	n.a $1,002	n.a $1,973
Medium Improvement Situation			
Award Rate	75%	64%	74%
Total Amt Awarded	(billion) $38.9	(billion) $1.9	(billion) $40.8
Total Amt Collected	(billion) $29.2	(billion) $1.1	(billion) $30.3
Collection Rate	75%	59%	74%
Mean Amt Collected *	$3,617	$1,294	$3,388

* These means are for custodial parents with awards.

Determining an Assured benefit: To determine the amount of assured benefit that each custodial family is entitled to receive, first of all, a guaranteed level of assurance should be established. Three different levels of assurance are simulated in this study in order to compare potential costs and benefits. They involve $1,000, $2,000, and $3,000 annually for the first child entitled to an assured benefit. In each plan, the benefit increases by $1,000 for the second child, $1,000 for the third, $500 for the fourth, and $500 for the fifth child.

   Given the plan of assured level, then, post private child support should be determined. The post private child support depends on an assumption of child support improvement under CSAS. Under the no improvement scenario in child support, the post amount of child support is equal to the estimated amount of current child support based on Eqt 4-6. Under the medium improvement scenario, the post child support amount is derived by using the Wisconsin percentage standard for a post award level and the collection rate predicted from Eqt 4-5 for each custodial family. In the Wisconsin percentage standard, the amount of child support award is determined by taking a certain percentage of the gross income of the absent parent, based on the number of children for whom that parent is responsible. The standard sets amounts at 17% of the absent parent's gross income for one child, 25% for two, 29% for three, 31% for four, and 34% for five or more children. Therefore, the amount of award is assigned to the family according to the number of eligible children and the income of the absent parent which is predicted from Garfinkel and Oellerich (1989)'s estimated equations. Once the amount of award is determined, the post amount of child support is then computed by utilizing the predicted rate of current collection. Since the medium improvement scenario implies a half-way increase in the collection rate, a child support payment under the medium improvement is calculated according to:

$$CS_{med} = AL_{post} * (E(CR) + 1)/2 \ \ ..... \ (Eqt \ 4\text{-}7)$$

where CS_{med} = increased payment of post child support under medium improvement; AL_{post} = post award level according to the Wisconsin formula; and $E(CR)$ = predicted collection rate.

   Finally, the public cost of an assured benefit is defined as a shortcoming of post child support received at the assured level for each of plans. For example, if the family is predicted to receive child support of $1,500 at the assured benefit of $2,000, the public cost of the assurance plan is $500. This public cost of assured benefit is subject to federal income tax in the simulation. As mentioned before, however, the proposed CSAS has some eligibility limits for assured benefits. First, the family must establish an award in order to be eligible for the assured benefit. Second, an either-or choice is required for AFDC families. A family on AFDC must leave the AFDC rolls in order to be entitled to the assured benefit. These constraints are taken into account when assured benefits are assigned for custodial families.

Changes in Health Care System

As addressed in chapter 3, this study looks at the benefit structure of the health care system. Simulating different health care systems in term of their structures of benefit requires a valuation method for health care. However, how to valuate medical care has been a controversial issue, because of its nature as an in-kind benefit. As the most common method, the market-value approach[19] is employed in this study to valuate Medicaid, employer-provided insurance, and national health insurance (NHI). The basic idea of the market-value approach is that a value of in-kind transfer is equal to its market cost of provision, implying that medical care transfers have worth for recipients equal to a cash transfer. More specific procedures for valuation will be described for each program (Medicaid, employer insurance, and NHI).

Valuation of Medicaid: The SIPP has information on whether or not a person was covered by Medicaid during the survey month. The SIPP also indicates the number of children in the family who were covered by Medicaid. Based on this information, Medicaid recipiency is identified for each family member. In addition, all AFDC cases are assumed to be covered by Medicaid, although some did not report Medicaid coverage.

To valuate Medicaid coverage, the mean expenditures of the state per AFDC child and per AFDC adult are utilized from a public source. The Green Book (1990) indicates the average Medicaid benefit expenditures per AFDC child and per AFDC adult in each state (p.1302). However, these means are overstated because they represent a recipient's value, and yet those eligible for Medicaid who did not receive any health care service also have certain value of coverage. To capture an adult's value based on eligibility, information is needed on the total number of eligible adults living with children under age 18 as well as on the total expenditures of Medicaid for this group in each state. Likewise, the total number of eligible children and total expenditures for the children group in each state are needed to obtain a children's value of Medicaid coverage. Unfortunately, the information on total eligible individuals and total expenditures available from public sources is not broken down for subgroups such as parents and children. Instead, the public source reports the percent of all eligible persons who were recipients of Medicaid in each state. Using this information, an eligible person's value is obtained with the recipient's value (that is, per AFDC adult value and per AFDC child value) multiplied by the percent of eligible individuals who were recipients in each of the states. The family value of Medicaid coverage is then the sum of child values and adult values. Thus, a family value of Medicaid varies over family size.

In the sample, some individuals reported Medicare coverage, although not many did. Persons reporting Medicare coverage are usually disabled or elderly.[20] Although those covered are a minor percentage in the sample, Medicare coverage is valuated in the following way. According to the Green Book (1991), the average annual benefit per person enrolled in 1988 was $1,626 for Part A (Hospital Insurance) and $1,070 for Part B (Supplementary Medical Insurance which is optional) (p.130-131). Since more than 98% of persons covered by Medicare have optional SMI coverage as well (see Green Book, 1991, pp.130-131), the HI mean benefit and the SMI mean benefit per enrollee are added together to capture a value of Medicare coverage which amounts to $2,696.

Valuation of Employer-Provided Health Insurance: Many working families are insured through employer-provided health coverage. To identify employer insurance coverage for each family member, three questions of the SIPP are utilized. The SIPP asked whether a person's health plan was provided through an employer or union. Also, the SIPP asked if the person was covered in his/her own name, somebody else's name, or both. These two sources are used to identify whether or not each person with an employed job in the family obtained health insurance through his/her employer. The SIPP further asked about the type of health insurance plan such as individual and family plans. If the employee obtained coverage through his/her employer under a family plan, his/her dependent spouse and children in the family are counted as insured individuals through employer coverage. If the employee has an individual plan, all dependents in the family are treated as those not covered through employer-based insurance.

When an employee is provided health insurance through his/her employer, the cost of purchasing insurance is met typically by both the employer and the employee. On the whole, a substantial percentage of the premium cost is paid by the employer. An employer contribution to health coverage can be considered as a compensation of work in the form of health care provision. Therefore, the amount of employer-paid premium is used to capture the value of private health coverage provided through the employer. However, information on employer-paid premium amounts is not available in the SIPP data.[21] Thus, an average employer-paid premium is substituted from a public source of health statistics. According to Gabel et al. (1989), the average monthly premium cost for a conventional plan was $93 ($1116/year) for an individual plan and $235 ($2820/year) for a family plan in 1988. The authors also indicate that the average percentage of premium paid by employers was 91% for the individual plan and 89% for the family plan. This means that employers on average paid $1016 annually for the individual plan and $2510 for the family plan.[22] These amounts of employer contribution are used for the value of employer insurance coverage. For instance, if a father obtained the family plan through his employer, $2510 is assigned as the family value of health coverage; and if he obtained the individual plan, employer insurance coverage is valued at $1016 for the family. This valuation method results in the mean family value of $2500 among families with employer-provided insurance.

However, this way of valuing employer insurance brings about problems of inconsistency with respect to Medicaid. First, Medicaid valuation takes account of family size. Second, Medicaid valuation differentiates values by age group by using values per AFDC adult and per AFDC child. On the other hand, the family value of employer-provided coverage as defined above depends only on the type of plan, considering neither family size nor age. To incorporate both family size and age into the values of employer insurance, per adult and per child values are derived as follows. First, the values of employer insurance in all covered families (defined above in terms of means of employer-paid premium) are aggregated to get the total value. The aggregated total value is $65 billion. Second, total adults and children covered through employer-based insurance are calculated. Total adults with employer insurance are estimated at 43.2 million, and total covered children at 40.7 million. Third, the ratio of per adult health expenditure to per child expenditure is utilized from public health statistics. According to Waldo et al.(1989), per capita health expenditure for 1987 was $1534 for adults aged between 19 and 64, and $745 for children under age 18. This indicates the ratio of 2.1 (i.e., 1534/745), implying that adults consume health services more than twice as much as children do. By putting all those figures together, finally, the values of employer insurance per adult and per child are generated by solving the following two equations:

(a) $AV_e = 2.1*CV_e$
(b) $AV_e*43.2 + CV_e*40.7 = 65000$ (unit in million)

where AV_e and CV_e are the per adult value and per child value of employer insurance coverage, respectively. The solution of these equations results in $971 per adult and $471 per child as the values of employer-based coverage. These values are used for each adult and child in the family who are identified with having employer insurance. Similar to Medicaid, then, the family value of employer insurance is the sum of all covered members' values in the family. As a result, the family values of employer insurance vary over family size. However, this adjustment for family size and age does not change the total value of employer insurance ($65 billion) or the mean value per family ($2500).

There are some families which report dual insurance coverage: some families with Medicaid as well as private health coverage; and some two-parent families in which both mother and father report employer-provided insurance coverage. Since extra coverage has almost a zero value, these families are assumed to choose the one coverage which provides the higher value.

Valuation of National Health Insurance (NHI): For National Health Insurance (NHI), it is proposed that current Medicaid and employer-provided health insurance be replaced with a single system, but people covered by Medicare will continue the current coverage under the

Medicare program. NHI is also proposed to cover all uninsured people in the sample including uninsured dependents of Medicare-covered individuals. The benefits offered under NHI would resemble the average benefit package under current employer-provided health insurance. Also, NHI is proposed to continue a similar cost-sharing including coinsurance and deductibles as in current employer insurance.

To valuate NHI coverage, the current mean of total premium cost for a family plan is employed. On average as of 1988, the total premium of $2820[23] was paid to purchase the family plan of private insurance. It should be noted that this cost of coverage reflects current benefit packages and cost-sharing features under private health insurance. Since the proposed NHI assumes similar benefit packages and cost-sharing, the use of the current premium (i.e., $2820) would not be far away from the cost required for NHI to cover a family.

However, an assignment of a flat amount ($2820) to each family as the family value of NHI again causes inconsistency problems in valuation methods, since family size and age are ignored. Therefore, NHI values per adult and per child are obtained according to the same adjustment procedure as in valuation of employer insurance. First, the family values of NHI ($2820 each family) are aggregated, resulting in $104 billion. Second, total adults (except those covered through Medicare) and total children are counted at 63.3 million and 68 million, respectively. Third, the ratio of per adult expenditure to per child expenditure under the current health care system--2.1--is again utilized. In other words, two equations are established as follows:

(a) $AV_n = 2.1*CV_n$
(b) $AV_n*63.3 + CV_n*68 = 103900$ (unit in million)

where AV_n = per adult value; and CV_n = per child value of NHI. The solution of these equations brings $1078 per adult and $524 per child as NHI values. These values are then assigned to each family member and summed to produce the family value of NHI. These adjusted values do not change either the aggregate total value ($104 billion) or the family mean value ($2820), but allow different values over family size and age category of family member.

Treatment of Current Employer-Paid Premiums under NHI: As mentioned before, current employer-provided insurance is proposed to be replaced with NHI. Therefore, NHI simulation needs to determine how to treat current premium costs paid by employers. In the long run, most economists predict that employers would shift the savings directly to workers by adjusting wages by the change in health benefit costs, holding workers' total compensation constant (Zedlewski et al., 1993, p.113). On this ground, the hourly compensation of current employer-paid premiums is computed and added to the current gross wage. This increased wage is used as the post wage rate under NHI simulation.

The hourly compensation of premium is calculated with the annual amount of employer-paid premium divided by the hours worked during the year. (Average compensation per hour is estimated at $0.79 among those with employed jobs who obtained employer insurance.[24]) This compensation per hour is then carried into the post wage in the following way: (a) for workers who obtained employer insurance coverage, the post wage is defined as the pre-wage rate plus the computed hourly compensation of employer-paid premiums; (b) for workers who had no employer-provided coverage, their post wages are the same as the pre-wages; and (c) for nonworkers, an hourly compensation of employer-paid premiums is imputed for the case that they would go to work in response to policy changes under the reform. The amount of employer-paid premium that current nonworkers would gain as a benefit once they decided to work, depends on the chance of getting employer-provided coverage and the type of plan selected (family or individual plan) given the employment. This can be stated as follows:

$$E(PREM) = P_{cov} * (P_{fp}*C_{fp} + P_{ip}*C_{ip}) \ ..... \ (Eqt \ 4-8)$$

where $E(PREM)$ is the predicted amount of employer-paid premium; P_{cov} is the probability of getting employer-provided insurance coverage; P_{fp} and P_{ip} are the probability of having the family plan and the individual plan, respectively; and C_{fp} and C_{ip} are the employer's premium cost for the family plan and the individual plan, respectively. To impute the employer-paid premium for nonworkers, the ideal way would be to estimate those probabilities (i.e., P_{cov}, P_{fp}, and P_{ip}). However, a simple way is adopted by substituting sample proportions. First, for the probability of getting employer insurance, sample proportions are generated separately by gender groups. In the sample, 78% of the employed fathers have employer-provided coverage; on the other hand, 51% of mothers with employed jobs are provided health insurance through their employers. These percentages could be substituted for the probability of getting employer insurance (P_{cov}) in Eqt 4-8.

However, the use of the mean proportions taken from the working groups is problematic for the group of nonworkers, because the nonworkers have certain characteristics different from the working group which constrain their possibilities of work. Therefore, those percentages are discounted by weighing the characteristics of nonworkers based on their average education level and the mean proportion of their marital status. Weighted mean percentages of obtaining employer insurance are 18% for nonworking mothers and 29% for nonworking fathers. Consequently, 18% and 29% are plugged into P_{cov} in Eqt 4-8 for nonworking mothers and fathers, respectively. Second, for the probability of having the family plan or the individual plan, the sample proportions are also adopted instead of an estimating procedure. The choice of family plan or individual plan is closely related to whether a person is the primary or secondary earner in the family. Percentages of having the family plan are thus generated separately for primary earners and secondary earners.[25] Among primary earners, 90% of those with employer insurance have the family plan. Among secondary earners, 78% of those with employer insurance have the family plan. Depending on primary or secondary earner, thus, .90 and .78 are plugged into P_{fp}; and residual fractions (i.e., .10 and .22) are plugged into P_{ip} in Eqt 4-8. Finally, amounts of employer premium cost for the family plan and the individual plan are needed for the variables C_{fp} and C_{ip} in Eqt 4-8. As described before, the average amounts of employer-paid premium cost are $2510 for the family plan and $1016 for the individual plan. These amounts are carried into C_{fp} and C_{ip} in Eqt 4-8. Once the amount of employer-paid premium is imputed for each nonworker, the hourly compensation is computed with that amount of premium divided by 2,000 hours of work. (Imputed compensations are averaged to $0.31 for nonworking fathers and $0.19 for nonworking mothers.) The post gross wage for a current nonworker is then defined as the estimated wage plus the imputed hourly compensation of employer's premium benefit. This imputation for post wage rate of nonworkers is needed to allow nonworkers to change labor supply status in response to proposed policy reform.

Financing Schedule for NHI Cost: To finance NHI cost, a payroll tax schedule is employed. Payroll taxes are known as a regressive taxation across income classes. However, the use of income tax schedules is held back because the cost of children's allowance is to be financed through income taxes. To reach a payroll tax rate for self-financing, I first obtain the total cost of national health insurance, and then gradually increase the payroll tax rate until the resulting tax revenue makes the program cost-neutral. In addition, some savings associated with NHI are incorporated into this process. A major source of savings is the current cost of Medicaid. Also, NHI is expected to bring additional income tax revenues as a result of converting currently tax-exempted employer contributions into increased wages. Other changes in income taxes and tax credits due to labor supply responses are also taken into account. With the associated savings, the resulting rate of payroll tax is 7.1%, which carries self-financing for the NHI cost of $104 billion.

Estimated Coverage Values: Table 4-7 presents health care coverage and estimated values under the current system and NHI. Under the current health care system, employer-based insurance covers the majority of parents and their children under the age of 18 (about 64%). Medicaid covers 11% of individuals living in families with children, and 12% are covered through self-purchased private insurance. After all current coverages are taken into account, about 15% of individuals in families with children are left without any type of medical coverage as of 1988.[26]

Table 4-7
Values Of Health Care Coverage

	People Covered (million)	Percent Covered (%) [*]	Total Value ($million)	Mean Value /Family ($)
Medicaid	14.6	11%	$10,746	[b] $2,321
Medicare	0.4	0.3%	$1,176	[c] $2,696
Employer Insurance	83.9	63.7%	$65,041	[d] $2,500
Self-Insured	15.7	12%	n.a	n.a
Uninsured	19.3	14.7%	n.a	n.a
NHI	131.7	100%	$104,121	[*] $2,821

Notes:

[*] This is the percent of persons covered under each type of health insurance plan; The sum may not be 100% because of some families with dual coverage, but for valuation, these families are assumed to be covered through the coverage that provides the higher value.

[b] For Medicaid values, state mean expenditures per AFDC adult (eligible) and per AFDC child (eligible) are used.

[c] For Medicare values, the sum of HI benefit and SMI benefit per enrollee is used; $2696 is the mean per enrollee (not per family).

[d] For values of employer insurance, employer-paid premiums are used.

[*] For values of NHI, average total premium costs currently to purchase private insurance coverage are used.

Table 4-7 also shows the aggregate totals and means of medical coverage values which result from the valuation methods described earlier. Medicaid values based on state mean expenditures per AFDC adult (eligible) and per AFDC child (eligible) results in a total value of $10.7 billion,[27] whose mean value is $2,321 per family covered. The use of employer-paid premiums for the value of employer insurance results in $65 billion for the total value and $2500 for the mean value per family covered through employer-based insurance. Also, the valuation of NHI based on current premium costs to purchase private health insurance brings the mean to $2821 per family and the total cost of $104 billion for providing universal coverage. Although Medicare coverage is a very marginal percentage in the sample, its total value amounts to $1.2 billion, with a mean of $2696 per enrollee.

Issue of Recipient Value of Health Care Coverage: Although it has been the most widely used of other alternative methods,[28] valuation of health care benefits based on their market costs has some flaws. The market value approach only consider the purchasing power of health benefits in the private market place. Because this method ignores an individual's own valuation of the worth of services received, the cost of purchasing health care services may not be equal to the recipient value. The recipient value is often measured by the amount of cash which would make the recipient just as well off as the in-kind benefit. In general, it is believed that the market value approach overstates the gain in the recipient's economic well-being (Wolfe and Moffitt, 1991). Some researchers have empirically shown that most in-kind benefits, especially medical transfers, are worth less to recipients than an equal dollar amount of cash transfer (Smeeding, 1975). If so, the market value of health care transfer should be discounted to reflect the recipient's own true value. However, existing research evidence shows a broad range of estimates for the recipient's cash-equivalent value. The estimated cash-equivalent values of medical benefits vary by type of program, income and other characteristics of the recipient, and the valuation approach. For instance, Smeeding (1975) estimated that, based on a normal expenditure approach, recipient values of cash equivalence (in 1972) were 63% for Medicaid, 93% for Medicare, and 78% for both programs. Altogether, including other estimates, Smeeding (1982) concluded that the recipient's relative values were between 58% and 74% of market value in terms of cash equivalence.

Since values of medical care coverage are treated as income sources in simulation, the results can be altered depending on how coverage value is determined. To test this sensitivity, I will discount health care values which are obtained in terms of market costs as described before. The rate of discount will be set at 0.58, which represents the lowest existing estimate for a cash equivalent value to the recipient. The choice of this low rate is to test the simulation results with the most conservative point of view.[29]

Determining Levels of Children's Allowance

Two levels of children's allowance are established and simulated. The first level of children's allowance is the amount that results from the current federal tax expenditures associated with the personal exemptions for children. To determine the initial level of allowance, I first calculate the additional revenue of income taxes from eliminating the exemptions for children, and then divide the revenue among all children. Second, all welfare savings are calculated including AFDC, food stamps, and Medicaid that would result from this initial level of allowance. The initial amount of children's allowance is subject to income taxes, which also brings an additional income tax revenue from the allowances themselves. The welfare savings and this income tax revenue from taxing allowances are additionally divided among all children.

From the SIPP sample, the total number of children is estimated at about 68 million. Total income tax savings from eliminating exemptions for children is estimated at $20.1 billion in 1988. If $20.1 billion is divided among the total number of children, the initial amount of allowance is estimated at about $296 per child. Also, if the welfare savings associated with this initial level and the tax revenue from the allowances themselves are incorporated, the level of children's allowance is increased to $409 per child. In addition, labor supply responses are taken into account for this level of children's allowance. This low level of allowance at $409 per child will be simulated as the conservative plan.

As a high level of children's allowance, $1000 per child for a year is simulated. This plan requires a gross cost of about 68 billion. To finance the cost, two sources of income tax system are utilized.

First, personal exemptions for children are eliminated as in the plan of $409. As mentioned above, the elimination of exemptions for children brings to the government the tax revenue of $20.1 billion. Second, an increase in income tax rates is employed to finance the rest of the cost ($47.9 billion). While the tax revenue associated with the repeal of exemptions for children can be estimated directly from my sample, the revenue from increased tax rates should be estimated from the whole population, because the sample includes only families with children under age 18 which is just a subset of population. To estimate from the whole population, some public sources of income-tax statistics are utilized. According to the U.S. Bureau of Census (1990, November, Table 1), the total number of all households paying income taxes was 74 million in 1988, with a mean income tax of $5,018. It is also reported that households with related children under the age of 18 which paid income taxes are numbered at 31 million in total, with an average income tax paid of $4,415. Using these figures, the total amount of income taxes collected from all households is calculated at $371 billion (74*5,018), and total income taxes collected from the households with children amount to $137 billion (31*4415). Dividing $137 billion by $371 billion results in 37% as the percentage of income taxes collected from families with children. Using this percentage, then, the total revenue collected from all households with increased tax rates would be as follows:

$$REV_{all} = REV_{smp}/0.37 \ ..... \ (Eqt \ 4\text{-}9)$$

where REV_{all} and REV_{smp} are tax revenues collected from all households and from households with children, respectively. For example, if an increase in tax rate by 1% in each tax bracket is estimated to collect $4 billion from the sample, then the total revenue collected from all households would be $10.8 billion (4/0.37). Based on Eqt 4-9, I then gradually increase the 1988 income tax rate in each tax bracket by a uniform percentage until the total revenue collected reaches cost-neutral with the residual cost of $47.9 billion for the plan of $1000. This process results in a 2.7% increase in the income tax rate to make the $1000 children allowance cost-neutral. Since allowances are subject to income taxes, the plan of $1000 would bring an additional tax revenue. Also, the plan would generate some welfare savings. In the same way as the $409 plan, these components of savings are incorporated into the process of establishing the cost-neutral rate of income tax increase. In addition, this process incorporates labor supply changes of the parent group due to increased income taxes, but ignores labor supply responses of all other groups.

Labor Supply Simulation Model

Selecting Empirical Utility Function: Analyzing the effects of policy changes requires a model which predicts behavioral responses to the changes in the tax and transfer system under the reform. To predict welfare participation and labor supply decisions, this study employs the adjusted utility formulation described in Garfinkel, Robins, Wong and Meyer (1990) which is based on the assumption of utility maximization. What follows is an outline of the model (Garfinkel et al, 1990; Meyer et al., 1991a; Meyer et al., 1991b).

The simulation requires specifying the form of utility functions, and obtaining estimates of the parameters of these functions (Meyer et al., 1991a, p. 14). For the functional specification, the Stone-Geary utility function, a well-known and often used form, is employed.[30] An augmented version of the Stone-Geary direct utility function is as follows (Garfinkel et al., 1990, p.12):

$$U(C,H) = (1-\beta)\ln(\frac{C}{m} - \delta) + \beta\ln(\alpha - \frac{H}{r})....(Eqt.4\text{-}10)$$

where C = annual consumption of market goods; H = annual hours of market work; β = marginal propensity to consume leisure (and thus $1-\beta$ = marginal propensity to consume market goods); δ = subsistence level of consumption; α = total annual time available for work; m & r = indexes that normalize C and H in accordance with the size and composition of the household. Eqt 4-10 is subject to the budget constraint:

$$C = N + WH ..... (Eqt.4\text{-}11)$$

where N and W are nonwage income and net wage rate, respectively. Maximization of Eqt 4-10 subject to Eqt 4-11 yields the following labor supply function for a person:[31]

$$H^* = \alpha(1-\beta)r - \frac{\beta(N-\delta m)}{W} \quad .....(Eqt.4-12)$$

Since a person's current observed labor supply will not, in general, be consistent with the utility-maximizing labor supply implied by Eqt 4-12,[32] an error term is appended to Eqt 4-12 to make the observed hours of work equal to the optimal hours of work (Garfinkel et al., 1990, p.13). The labor supply function including the error term is then:

$$H = \alpha(1-\beta)r - \frac{\beta(N-\delta m)}{W} + \varepsilon .....(Eqt.4-13)$$

As Moffitt (1986) and Hausman (1985) have noted, the error term (ε) in general can be thought of as representing a combination of measurement error, optimization error, and unmeasured heterogeneity. For the purposes of this study, however, the error term is assumed to arise only from unmeasured heterogeneity, because of assumptions that observed hours of work are equal to the optimal hours of work[33] and that the decision to participate in the post-programs is based on utility maximization. Treating an error term in this manner causes problems in simulating the labor supply response for non-workers (noninterior solutions) (Garfinkel et al., 1990, p.13). Since they are not generally on the margin of going to work, the optimal hours of work for nonworkers are assumed to be negative even though the observed hours of work are zero. To deal with this problem empirically, it is assumed that the error term is distributed normally with a mean of zero and a standard deviation of 990 hours per year.[34] An error term is then randomly selected from a truncated normal distribution to ensure that the optimal hours of work are less than or equal to zero.

Finally, having incorporated an error term, the adjusted utility function optimally maximized at the observed hours is derived as follows: For a female-headed family (Garfinkel et al, 1990),

$$U(C,H,\varepsilon) = (1-\beta)\ln(\frac{C}{m} - \delta) + \beta\ln(\alpha - \frac{H}{r} + \frac{\varepsilon}{r(1-\beta)}) ....(Eqt.4-14)$$

For a married couple family (Meyer et al., 1991b),[35]
where

$$U(C,H_1,H_2,e_1,e_2)=(1-\beta_1-\beta_2)\ln(\frac{C}{m}-\delta)+\beta_1\ln(Z_1)+\beta_2\ln(Z_2)(Eqt.4-15)$$

$$Z_1=\alpha_1-\frac{H_1}{r_1}+\frac{(1-\beta_2)e_1}{r_1(1-\beta_1-\beta_2)}+\frac{\beta_1 W_2 e_2}{r_1 W_1(1-\beta_1-\beta_2)}$$

$$Z_2=\alpha_2-\frac{H_2}{r_2}+\frac{(1-\beta_1)e_2}{r_2(1-\beta_1-\beta_2)}+\frac{\beta_2 W_1 e_1}{r_2 W_2(1-\beta_1-\beta_2)}$$

Garfinkel et al. (1990) and Meyer et al. (1991b) did not estimate the parameters of this model, but utilized the estimates from the existing labor supply literature. In particular, these studies adopted the parameters estimated by Johnson and Pencavel (1984) in their analysis of the labor supply response to the Seattle and Denver Income Maintenance Experiments (SIME-DIME). For single-female headed families, adopted parameters based on Johnson and Pencavel's long-run estimates are: $\beta = 0.128$; $\alpha = 2151$; $\delta = -2776$; $r= 1- 0.071*P$ (where $P = 1$ if preschool child(ren) are present); and $m= 1 - 0.401*ln(1 + K)$, where K is the number of children. For families of husband and wife, parameter estimates are: $\beta_1 = 0.2113$; $\beta_2 = 0.1238$; $\alpha_1 = 2587$; $\alpha_1 = 2012$; $\delta = -1616$; $r_1 = 1$; $r_2 = 1 - 0.051*P$ (where $P= 1$ if preschool child(ren) are present); and $m= 1 + 1.069*ln(1 + K)$, where K is the number of children. Unfortunately, Johnson and Pencavel (1984) did not estimate parameters for single-male headed families. Since the sample includes single-father families (132 cases), these families are constrained not to change their labor supply and program participation under the reform.

Preparing Variables in Labor Supply and Utility Functions: Once utility function and parameters are established, variables involved the equations must be prepared. As seen in Eqt 4-13, predicting the optimal hours of work (H') requires variables of unearned income (N), net wage rate (W_1 & W_2 for head of household and wife if present), presence of preschool child(ren) (P), and the number of children in each family

(*K*). Given the predicted optimal hours of work (*H*'), a variable of the observed hours (*H*) is further needed to derive the error term (that is, error term (ε) = observed hours - optimal hours). Besides these variables, calculating utility in Eqt 4-14 and Eqt 4-15 requires the amount of annual consumption available after taxes (*C*). Variables such as the presence of preschool child(ren) (*P*) and the number of children in the family (*K*) are easier to define because the SIPP data reported this information. The other variables, however, such as observed hours (*H*), unearned income (*N*), and net wage rate (*W*), must be produced by using first-hand information available in the data. More details will be described separately for each variable needed.

Annual Hours of Work Observed (H): The SIPP provides only monthly information. As described earlier, total monthly hours worked in all jobs are obtained by using reported information in the SIPP. However, labor supply and utility equations require annual terms. There are two possible ways to obtain annual terms. First, monthly information from the SIPP can be merged to cover the length of time of 12 months before and after September 1988. Annual hours worked are then the sum of hours worked in each of the twelve months. The second way of obtaining annual terms is to multiply the monthly information of September of 1988 by 12. Although the first method captures more accurate picture of the year, the second method is adopted, primarily because merging different months results in a problem of sample truncation (some cases exit and new cases enter over time). Thus, for this study, the annual hours of work currently observed is defined as the total hours of work during September multiplied by 12.

Annual Consumption (C): An annual amount of consumption is also required in Eqt 4-14 and Eqt 4-15. The annual term of consumption is obtained by the monthly income multiplied by 12 in the same way of annual hours of work. The amount of consumption in the simulation is defined as the net income of the family available for consumption of goods after all taxes are paid out during the year. According to this definition, the gross income in each of the families is first calculated by adding up all sources of income figured in the previous steps. In other words, the gross income is the sum of earnings, AFDC benefit, child support received, amount of EITC, cash values of in-kind benefits including food stamps, Medicaid, and employer-provided insurance coverage, and all other taxable or nontaxable incomes.[36] The amount of taxes is calculated from federal income and payroll taxes figured for each family. The net income is then the gross income minus the total amount of taxes.

Net Wage (W) and Unearned Income (N): The labor supply model also requires an hourly net wage and an unearned income. To prepare these variables, an exact budget line must be modelled. Normally, the net wage rate would be represented by the slope of the line in each segment of budget sets, and the unearned income would be represented by the intercept (i.e., virtual income) associated with each segment when the segment line is projected to zero hours of work. However, the use of exact budget sets is difficult because of many kinks involved in taxes and transfers. It has been noted that the budget line itself has many kinks even without considering AFDC. Inclusion of AFDC, EITC, and values of food stamps, Medicaid, and employer insurance coverage makes it virtually impossible to establish the exact budget line because of the interactions of transfers as well as taxes. For this reason, the net wage rate and the unearned income for each of families are produced according to the following procedures rather than by the use of budget sets.

By definition, a net wage per hour means an additional net income returned after taxes if a person works one additional hour. This can be stated as follows:

$$W_1 = C(H_1 + 1, H_2) - C(H_1, H_2)$$
$$W_2 = C(H_1, H_2 + 1) - C(H_1, H_2) \ldots \ldots \ (Eqt \ 4\text{-}16)$$

where W = net wage rate; C = net family income at current hours worked; and H = current hours worked. The subscript 1 stands for the head of family and the subscript 2 for the wife if present. Based on the equations, first, the net family income at the currently observed hours worked is calculated as described above. Second, a person in the family is assumed to work one more hour given the current gross wage rate. If he/she works one additional hour, his/her earnings would increase. As the earnings increase, some other sources of income and taxes would change accordingly. For example, AFDC and food stamp benefits would decrease as the earnings increase; and income and payroll taxes would increase. Given the increased earnings at one additional hour, thus, AFDC, food stamps, and Medicaid (because all AFDC cases are assumed to be recipients of Medicaid), EITC, and income and payroll taxes are recalculated. The new net family income at the one additional hour is then obtained according to the same procedure as for the current net income. Finally, the net wage is calculated with the net family income at the one additional hour minus the net family income at the current hours. For instance, for a single mother who works 1,000 hours during the year, the net wage is her would-be net income at 1,001 minus her net income at 1,000.

Unearned income is also computed in the following way:

$$N = C(H_1, H_2) - W_1H_1 - W_2H_2 \quad ..... \quad (Eqt \ 4-17)$$

where N = unearned income for the family; and other variables are the same as in Eqt 4-16. For single-parent families, wife variables such as W_2 and H_2 do not enter in Eqt 4-16 and Eqt 4-17.

Given the set of variables prepared above, the current utility is computed according to Eqt 4-14 and Eqt 4-15 depending on the type of family. The resulting current utility will serve as the baseline for a comparison with the post-reform situation.

Simulating Labor Supply Responses under Post Reform

Specifying Points of Hours to Be Compared: To predict changes in program participation and labor supply under the post reform on the ground of utility maximization, the post utility should be generated. Since an exact budget line has the difficulty of too many kinks as mentioned above, an alternative approach is employed, in which the post utility is computed at a specified number of hours worked.[37] Checking various points of hours can resolve the problem of establishing an exact line of post budget sets under the reform program(s).

A comparison of current utility with post utility levels can be made at every hour of work. For example, we could compute post-reform utility at every hour between 0 and 60 per week, and compare each of these points with the current utility. However, this process requires much computing time. Given this constraint of computing time, thus, a certain specified number of points are selected. For men, we know that few working men work part time. Therefore, the post utility among men is calculated at every 5 hours between 0 and 30, and between 50 and 60, but every hour between 30 and 50 per week. For women, the post utility is computed at every hour (per week) for five hours below and above the number of hours that each woman currently works, and every 5 hours elsewhere.[38] Since utility function requires an annual hours of work, the point of weekly hours specified in this way is converted to annual terms.

Checking post-utility in this way can have the disadvantage of getting quite inaccurate results in areas of kink points (Meyer et al., 1991b, p.487). However, it allows both the interaction of all current programs and the interaction of current and post-reform programs. Furthermore, as discussed in Meyer et al. (1991b), this approach can reflect the real world more accurately than the traditional model, because people cannot choose just any number of hours of work but must choose among a discrete numbers of hours (p.487).

Computing Post Utility: The next step after defining each point of hours worked per year is computing the post utility at that point. The same procedures are applied as for the current utility. The post earnings at that point of hours is calculated, assuming that gross wages are constant across all hours. As the earnings change, amounts of AFDC and food stamps are recalculated accordingly. EITC and taxes are further recalculated according to the post level of earnings at that point of hours. It should be noted that some new sources of income are entered, and some of the current income sources vanish as a result of implementing policy changes. The family gross income under the reform includes child support assurance, children's allowance, and a value of national insurance in place of the values of Medicaid and employer insurance. Taxes also change: personal exemptions for children are eliminated and an increased rate of income tax is imposed to finance the children's allowance; an additional payroll tax rate is levied for the cost of national health insurance. By incorporating these changes under the reform, all variables required to compute the post utility at the specified hours are prepared following the same procedures as described before for the current utility. In calculation of post utility based on Eqt 4-14 and Eqt 4-15, the hours of work (H) is the specified number of hours in the place of current hours. The net consumption (C) is the gross income (including an assured benefit, a children's allowance, and the value of national insurance, besides the post earnings, AFDC and food stamps calculated at the point of hours) minus post taxes levied by new tax schedules. At each point of hours, a net wage (W) and an unearned income (N) are also calculated in the same way as for the current utility. Using the variables prepared at the specified number of hours, finally, the post utility is computed at that point.

Predicting Post Program Participation and Labor Supply: A behavioral change responding to the reform is determined on the basis of utility maximization. To do this, the highest post utility is selected from all points of specified hours, and then the highest post utility is compared with the current utility. If the highest point of post utility is greater than the current utility, the family is assumed to change to that point of hours. Otherwise, the family is assumed to remain at the current situation. Once the maximizing point of hours is selected simultaneously for a head of family and a wife (if present), AFDC and food stamps benefit levels are determined according to the level of family earnings at the selected hours. The gross income and taxes are determined accordingly, and the net family income is finally obtained at that point of hours.

As the final step, these predictions of income, taxes, program participation, and hours of work for an individual family are carried to generate the aggregate effects of the post reform on certain final outcomes. Indeed, all previous steps described in this methods section have been prepared to produce the final outcome variables by which the post reform is compared with the current system. Those variables are: (a) effects on poverty incidence and gap; (b) effects on welfare participation and expenditures including AFDC, food stamps, and Medicaid; (c) impacts on income redistribution; (d) effects on labor supply; and (e) gross and net costs of the proposed program(s). A comparison of the post reform with the current system is made for each of these outcome variables. How to define the measures of these variables will be described in chapter 5.

Notes

1. From the data dictionary of topical modules, it is not clear for the universe of child support questions whether mothers who had no children from the most recent divorce but had children from an earlier divorce, or remarried mothers who had children out of wedlock were included. From a conversation with a data consultant in the Census Bureau, I found that those mothers are not captured in the topical module unless they obtained child support agreements or child support payments.

2. According to the 1989 Green Book (p.555), AFDC average monthly caseloads as of 1988 were 3.75 million. Total AFDC cases who reported recipiency in the sample are 2.6 million, indicating 30% underreporting.

3. In calculation of AFDC benefit amounts, the first $50 of child support received is disregard; the earnings are taxed by estimated tax rate (provided by Fraker et al. [1985]); and all other income sources are taxed at 100%.

4. According to the 1989 Green Book (p.555), AFDC average monthly caseloads in 1988 were 3.75 million, benefit payments amounted to $16.8 billion, and child support collections were $1.4 billion.

5. For a family with an elderly or disabled member, CMI_b computation is a little different: there is no ceiling of $170 and medical costs exceeding $35 are subtracted.

6. A few states (e.g., Alaska, Hawaii, Guam, and Virgin Islands) have different deductions and larger maximums, but I ignore them for simplification.

7. According to the 1990 Green Book (p. 1252), only 85% of AFDC cases receive food stamps as well. Automatic assignment of all AFDC cases to food stamp recipiency could result in an overestimated number of food stamp families. Thus, only AFDC cases who reported food stamp recipiency are considered as receiving food stamps as well.

8. The 1990 Green Book indicates that 5.8 million households were on the food stamp program with total expenditures of about $12 billion in 1988. These figures, however, are not comparable with my estimates because households other than families with children are included. However, the Green Book reports that 61% of all food stamp households were families with children in 1987. By using this percentage, the number of families with children which receive food stamps is calculated at 3.5 million as of 1988, which is almost identical with my estimate. Unfortunately, the Green Book does not provide the percent of expenditures received by families with children. If adopting the same percentage (61%), total benefit expenditures for these families would be $7.3 billion, which is again identical with my estimate.

9. That is, the monthly number of hours worked in each of the jobs (if more than one) is first calculated by the hours worked per week times the number of weeks worked on that job. The total hours of work per month on all jobs is the sum of monthly hours worked in each of the jobs.

10. LAMBDA term is ignored in this calculation.

11. Wage = EXP(Logwage + StdError^2/2).

12. State income taxes are ignored.

13. This estimate is slightly below the public figure of total EITC. The 1990 Green Book (p.837) indicates $4.8 billion for the total amount of credits and $527 for the average credit per family.

14. The taxable income includes income from earnings, assets, sick pay, alimony, pensions, life insurance amounts, income from roomers, GI benefits, and reserve pay. The following sources of income are counted as non-taxable: AFDC, unemployment, social security, railroad retirement, SSI, veterans payments, Worker's compensation, general assistance and other welfare, and foster care.

15. The 1988 tax rates and brackets are as follows:
For joint filing status, 15% if the adjusted gross income (AGI) is less than or equal to $29750; 28% ($29750 < AGI <= $71900); 33% ($71900 < AGI <= $149250) and 28% (AGI > $149250). For

single filing status, 15% (AGI <= $17850); 28% ($17850 < AGI <= $43150); 33% ($43150 < AGI <= $89560) and 28% (AGI > $89560).

16. Self-employment tax credits phased out through 1989. See the Green Book (1989), p.120.

17. See Meyer, Garfinkel, Robins, and Oellerich (1991a).

18. Estimated coefficients are taken from Garfinkel and Oellerich (1989), but see Oellerich (1984) for more details of estimating procedures.

19. I avoid using the term of 'government cost' approach, since private health insurance is included for valuation as well. However, it should be noted that some economists, for example Smeeding and Moon (1980), used 'market value' and 'government cost' for medical benefits interchangeably.

20. Some puzzling cases are found in the sample. Some reported having Medicare coverage who are neither over the age of 65 nor disabled. These cases are treated as misreporting.

21. The SIPP asked whether the employer paid the full cost of premium, part cost, or none. However, this information is not enough to know the exact amount of employer contribution, because premium amounts vary, particularly over the size of firm.

22. The rest of the cost is paid by the employee with the plan. Those with the individual plan paid $100, and those with the family plan paid $310 on average during the year.

23. This premium cost includes employer-paid and employee-paid premiums.

24. The U.S. Bureau of Labor Statistics (1988) indicates that the average employer cost of insurance per hour worked for all workers in private industry was $0.78 as of March 1988. Since the Bureau counted all insurance provisions, an hourly compensation of employer costs only for the health insurance provision should be lower than $0.78.

However, the Bureau included all workers in calculating the average cost per hour, while only workers covered through their employers are included in my calculation. This may contribute to the higher estimate in this study, compared to the Bureau's estimate.

25. If both parents are working, I assume that mother is the secondary earner in the family.

26. A small number of families have dual coverage. Thus, these percentages are not summed to 100%. For valuation, however, these families are treated as choosing the one coverage which provides the higher value.

27. According to Green Book (1991, p.1427), total Medicaid payments in 1988 to children under age 21 and adults in families with dependent children were $11.7 billion. Since my sample includes children under age 18 and their parents, my estimate is lower than this total expenditure.

28. They include the cash-equivalent method (e.g., Smeeding[1975], Smeeding & Moon[1980], Smolensky et al.[1977], and Cooper & Katz[1978]); the fund-released approach (e.g., Kraft and Olsen [1977], Weinberg[1981]); and the poverty budget share method (Smeeding & Moon [1980]). As a variant of the market-value method, family-specific index valuation has been suggested by Wolfe and Moffitt (1991).

29. Food stamp imputation previously described is also based on the market value approach. However, the value of food stamps is more easily measured by their face value. Thus, the range of estimated recipient's values is much smaller and much closer to the market purchasing power than for medical care. For instance, Smeeding (1982) indicated the range of 83% to 97% for a relative value to the recipient. For this reason, market values of food stamps are used without discounting.

30. For a discussion of the properties of this function, see Goldberger (1967).

31. For a married couple, labor supply function has a different form. It is derived as follows:

$$H_1^* = \alpha_1(1-\beta_1)r_1 - \frac{\beta_1(N-\delta m + \alpha_2 W_2 r_2)}{W_1}$$

$$H_2^* = \alpha_2(1-\beta_2)r_2 - \frac{\beta_2(N-\delta m + \alpha_1 W_1 r_1)}{W_2}$$

where the subscript 1 indicates the husband's and the subscript 2 indicates the wife's (Meyer et al., 1991b, p.486).

32. This labor supply equation can be used to derive income and wage elasticities. The total income elasticity is given by:

$$E_n = \frac{\partial H}{\partial N} * W = -\beta$$

and the uncompensated wage elasticity is given by:

$$E_w = \frac{\partial H}{\partial W} * \frac{W}{H} = \frac{\beta(N-\delta m)}{WH}$$

The uncompensated wage elasticity minus the total income elasticity equals the compensated wage elasticity (Garfinkel et al., 1990, p.12).

33. In order to make the observed hours equal to the optimal hours, the error term is defined as the observed hours minus optimal hours predicted by Eqt 4-12.

34. This standard deviation is taken from Keely et al.(1978), since Johnson and Pencavel (1984) do not present such an estimate in their study.

35. Garfinkel et al. (1990) do not specify utility formulation for a two-parent family. Thus, utility formulation for a two-parent family is adopted from Meyer et al. (1991b).

36. Other taxable income includes income from assets, sick pay, alimony, pensions, life insurance amounts, income from roomers, GI benefits, and reserve pay. Other non-taxable income includes income from unemployment insurance, social security, railroad retirement, SSI, veterans payments, Worker's compensation, general assistance and other welfare, and foster care.

37. The approach was originally developed in the work of Meyer et al. (1991b). They checked every ten hours between 0 and 60 per week.

38. For example, if she currently works 25 hours per week, checking points would be 0, 5, 10, 15, 20, 21, 22, 23, 24, 26, 27, 28, 29, 30, 35, ... so on and 55, 60.

V

Results

This chapter presents the results for costs and effects of policy changes. To compare the current regime, dominated with income-tested programs, with the non-income-tested regime, all income sources and taxes are figured out under the current regime and under the post regime, respectively. By aggregating these individual variables, the following outcomes are produced: (a) effects on poverty incidence and gap; (b) effects on welfare participation and expenditures including AFDC, food stamps and Medicaid; (c) impacts on income redistribution; (d) effects on labor supply; and (e) gross and net costs of the proposed program(s).

Under each of these dimensions, for a comparison, four sets of simulation are presented. The first three sets include the results from simulating a single program--child support assurance, children's allowance, and national health insurance, respectively. For CSAS alone, four alternatives for an assured level are simulated: zero; $1000; $2000; $3000 (for the first child). A zero level of assurance represents the effects of CSAS components except an assured benefit (i.e., the effects of private child support collection). Since the CSAS effects are affected by the performance of private child support, two assumptions are adopted. The most pessimistic scenario assumes no improvement in current award incidence, award levels, and collections of child support (no improvement scenario). A more realistic scenario involves medium improvement in child support dimensions by half the distance from the current to the perfect system (medium improvement scenario). Therefore, two panels of each table present the results from these scenarios under the single CSAS simulation. For the single program of children's allowance, two levels of allowance are simulated, one plan of $409 and the other of $1000 per child. As a reminder, the allowance of $409 is determined by eliminating tax deductions for children; and the level of $1000 is associated with an increase in income tax rates by 2.7% in addition to eliminating exemptions. The national health insurance is also separately simulated according to the structure of plan described in the methods chapter. These runs of single program are intended to separate the combined effects from a single program's effects.

The final set involves simulation of all-combined programs. For simulation of the combined regime, three programs are included: CSAS (at assured level of $2000); children allowance (at $1000); and national health insurance. Since CSAS is affected by the assumption of private child support, two scenarios (no improvement and medium improvement) are simulated for the combined run as well.

Effects on Poverty

Definition of Poverty Measures: To capture the effects on poverty of the proposed reform, two measures of poverty are employed--poverty rate and poverty gap. Under both of the current regime and the post regime, the poverty status of each family is determined according to the official poverty lines by family size.[1] The poverty cutoff corresponding to the family size is then compared with a family's income. If the income of the family falls below its threshold, all persons in the family are classified as poor. And these poor people are aggregated to generate the rate of poverty incidence under the current system and the post reform, respectively. The denominator of the poverty rate is the weighted total number of people in the sample; the numerator is the weighted total number of people who are defined as poor. As a measure of the effects on poverty, then, a percentage change in the poverty rate is calculated as follows:

$$PCTCHG_a = 100*(R_2 - R_1)/R_1$$

where $PCTCHG_a$ = percent change in poverty rate; R_1 = current poverty rate; and R_2 = post poverty rate.

For a second measure of poverty, the poverty gap is computed for each of the families defined as poor. The poverty gap is the amount of income required to raise the income of a poor family up to the poverty level. In other words, the poverty gap is the difference between the income and the official poverty line for a family in poverty. By summing up these gaps in those families who are below the poverty threshold, the aggregate poverty gap is generated separately under the current situation and the post-reform situation. Finally, a percent change in poverty gap due to the reform is derived in a similar way to the percent change in poverty rate:

$$PCTCHG_b = 100*(G_2 - G_1)/G_1$$

where $PCTCHG_b$ = percent change in poverty gap; G_1 = current poverty gap; and G_2 = post poverty gap.

For all poverty measures, a family income under the current system is defined as all cash incomes including child support received, AFDC benefits, and cash values of in-kind benefits such as food stamps, Medicaid, and employer-provided insurance, and subtracts income and payroll taxes. It should be noted that official poverty rates published for every year since 1959 have been computed on a different income definition. Neither in-kind benefits like food stamps, Medicare, Medicaid, and employer-provided health insurance are included, nor are taxes paid subtracted in its income definition. Therefore, my estimates of current poverty rate and gap (will be presented below) are not comparable with published official estimates.

Results for Effects on Poverty Rate and Poverty Gap: Table 5-1 presents the results for poverty effects of the post-reform program(s). With the income definition (described above), 15.4 million people living in families with children under age 18 are in poverty, indicating a poverty rate of 11.7%; and the aggregate poverty gap of those poor families is $14.3 billion in 1988 dollars.

Under the post reform, the percent changes in poverty rate and poverty gap due to a single program of child support assurance (CSAS) under different assumptions of child support are as follows (see Table 5-1, panels 1 & 2). If there is no improvement in child support, the assured benefit alone shows only a small impact on poverty. Under the no improvement assumption, the modest level of assured benefit ($2000) is predicted to decrease the number of poor people only by 1.9%; the poverty gap by 2.5%. Even at the high level ($3000) using the same assumption, the anti-poverty effects of CSAS alone are still low--4.2% and 4.0% of reduction in poverty rate and gap, respectively. As mentioned before, it is more realistic to expect some improvement in the private child support situation particularly because of the income withholding and incentive provisions of CSAS. The use of a percentage standard for award levels and the increased rates of award and collection explain a large portion of the anti-poverty effects of CSAS. A medium improvement in child support without assured benefits is estimated to reduce the rate of poverty by 6.7% and the gap by 7.2% (see zero level of assurance in the second panel). The CSAS of $2000 with medium improvement would reduce the number of poor people by 8% and the gap by 9%. At the $3000 plan with this optimistic assumption, however, the anti-poverty effects of CSAS are not large: at most, a 10% reduction in people in poverty and 11% reduction in poverty gap.

A caution is needed regarding my estimates for the anti-poverty effects of CSAS. One purpose for simulating each of the single programs is to separate the single effect from the combined effect. For this reason, I include all families for CSAS simulation, although CSAS is relevant only for a subset of the sample--custodial families. Since single parents are more likely to be poor, percent reductions in the poverty rate and gap under CSAS would be larger than those estimates if the sample were restricted to custodial families. I will present the anti-poverty effects of CSAS among custodial families in the final section of this chapter.

Under the single program of children's allowance, the effects on poverty and income indicate that the low level of $409 per child does not achieve much impact, whereas the high level of allowance ($1000 per child) plays a significant role as a means of reducing poverty (see Table 5-1, panel 3 of post reform). At the $409 plan, the poverty incidence is estimated to decrease by 3.1% and poverty gap by 8.2%. On the other hand, the children allowance of $1000 would take 15.3% of poor people out of poverty and reduce the gap by 21.6%. These estimates under the $1000 allowance are larger than their counterparts under the same level of CSAS: the estimated decline of the poverty rate (15.3%) under the $1000 allowance is more than twice as large as the 7% decline predicted under CSAS ($1000) with the medium improvement assumption; and the estimated reduction in the poverty gap (21.6%) due to the $1000 allowance is almost three times higher than the 7.7% reduction under CSAS ($1000 and medium). These results indicate that the children allowance has more potential as a means for decreasing poverty. This is simply because it benefits more children, including those not relevant for child support as well. However, it should be remembered that this larger effectiveness of the children allowance ($1000) on poverty is obtained at the cost of raising income tax rates by 2.7%.

The estimated effects of the single program of NHI on poverty are greater than those under the CSAS or children's allowance (see Table 5-1, panel 4 of post reform). The NHI alone is predicted to reduce the number of poor people by about 23% and the poverty gap by more than 32%. Among those out of poverty under NHI, the currently uninsured account for 72%. This indicates how much the current health care system has disfavored the poor through a limited access to coverage, although Medicaid has provided a safety net of health care. It should be noted that health care benefits as well as increased payroll taxes for financing NHI are taken into account in the poverty measures. Even if payroll taxes are not exempted for the poor, the results demonstrate that the anti-poverty effects of NHI can be still maintained through the universal benefit structure.

The final panel of Table 5-1 shows the estimated anti-poverty effects under the non-income-tested regime. Implementation of the three programs all together indicates that poverty among families with children would be substantially cut down. Assuming medium improvement in private child support, the poverty rate is estimated to decline by 51% and the poverty gap by more than 61%. Even under the pessimistic assumption, the three-combined programs perform significant anti-poverty effects: a 43% decrease in poverty incidence and a 54% reduction in poverty gap.

Table 5-1
Effects On Poverty

Pre Reform	People in Poverty (million)	Poverty Gap (billion)
	15.4	$14.3

Post Reform	% Chg in People	% Chg in Gap
CSAS (Under Current Child Support System)		
1000	-0.5	-1.1
2000	-1.9	-2.5
3000	-4.2	-4.0
CSAS (Under Medium Improvement)		
0	-6.7	-7.2
1000	-7.0	-7.7
2000	-8.0	-9.0
3000	-10.0	-11.1
Children Allowance		
409	-3.1	-8.2
1000	-15.3	-21.6
National Health Insurance		
NHI	-22.6	-32.3
Three Programs Combined: CSAS($2000), CA($1000) & NHI		
Under Current	-42.9	-54.2
Under Medium	-50.6	-61.4

Notes: The current child support system assumes no improvement in private child support; Medium improvement assumes establishing award levels by the Wisconsin standard and increasing award and collection rates by half the distance from the current to the perfect system; CA of $409 is cost neutral with eliminating exemptions for children and CA of $1000 is cost neutral with raising the income tax rate by 2.7% in addition to exemptions eliminated; For NHI financing, payroll tax rate is increased by 7.08%.

Effects on Welfare Participation and Expenditures

Proposed non-income-tested transfers are expected to reduce welfare participation and expenditures. Three welfare programs are included for this regard: AFDC, food stamps, and Medicaid. Because of the current benefit package closely links these three together, the effects of the reform on these welfare programs are estimated simultaneously.

Defining Measures of Welfare Effects: To measure the extent of reductions in welfare participation, two outcome variables are employed: (a) percent change in caseloads; and (b) percent change in benefit expenditures. The calculating procedure for a percent change is the same as in the anti-poverty measures previously described. The first measure is to count how many cases would exit AFDC, food stamps, or Medicaid programs under the reform. A percent change in caseloads is the percent of those off-cases for each program.

The second measure is to count the benefit savings of the welfare program due to the reform. AFDC benefit savings, for instance, could be generated from two sources. First, if the case is predicted to move off the AFDC roll, the savings equal the current amount of AFDC receipt. Second, the case may not leave AFDC, but the benefit amount may reduce because of new sources of income or increased earnings under the post program(s). For this type of case, the AFDC savings is defined as the difference between current and post benefit amounts. The same procedure is applied to figure the savings of food stamps. However, the savings of Medicaid are counted only from cases which move off AFDC and lose Medicaid recipiency. The percent change in expenditures is the percent of the benefit savings in each welfare program cost.

Results for Effects on AFDC: Table 5-2 presents the effects of the reform program(s) on caseloads and expenditures of AFDC, food stamps, and Medicaid, respectively. Under the current system, families with children on the AFDC program totalled 3.8 million, receiving benefit payments amounting to $16.1 billion in 1988 dollars.

As expected, the single reform of CSAS is estimated to decrease AFDC caseloads and to bring benefit savings (see Table 5-2, cols. 1 & 2, panels 1 & 2 of post reform). Under the medium improvement scenario, the CSAS of $0 assured level represents the effects of private child support when the percentage standard is adopted for award levels, and award and collection rates are increased by half to the perfect system. A medium improvement in child support (without assured benefits) is predicted to decrease AFDC caseloads by 7.5% and AFDC benefit expenditures by 13.1%. Adding an assured benefit to CSAS enables more AFDC cases to exit the AFDC program, but its impact is not large: AFDC caseloads would further decrease by 0.4 percentage points at the $1000 assured benefit level (a 7.9% decrease); 0.9 percentage points at the $2000 level (a 8.4% decrease); and 3.7 percentage points at the $3000 level (11.2%). Under the same scenario, CSAS would decrease AFDC payments by the range of 13% to 14%, depending on levels of assurance. As seen in Table 5-2, AFDC payments decrease at a faster rate than AFDC cases do, suggesting that assured benefits may be not enough to take custodial parents out of welfare.

The most pessimistic assumption of child support would provide more conservative estimates for the CSAS's effects on AFDC. Without improvement in child support, the assured benefit would only have a trivial effect on AFDC participation: only a 1% reduction in caseloads at the $2000 level; a 3.5% reduction at the $3000 level; and almost a negligible impact at the $1000 level. Estimated declines in AFDC expenditures are less than 1% at all levels of assured benefit with current child support. In contrast to the medium improvement scenario, predicted effects on caseloads are larger than on payments under no improvement. This is primarily because of AFDC cases whose benefits are relatively small. These cases tend to quickly move off due to assured benefits, but contribution of these cases to benefit savings is relatively marginal because of their small amounts.

The single program of children's allowance is also predicted to decrease the number of AFDC families and benefit expenditures (see Table 5-2, cols. 1 & 2, panel 3 of post reform). The allowance of $409 alone, whose level is cost neutral with replacing income tax deductions for children, would reduce AFDC rolls by about 5% and save AFDC expenditures by about 17%. The allowance plan of $1000, which requires a 2.7% raise in income tax rate as well as replaces deductions for children, would decrease AFDC caseloads by 13% and benefit payments by about 39%. Compared with the $1000 assured benefit, the same amount of children's allowance ($1000) is predicted to create larger reductions in AFDC caseloads: 7.9% (under medium improvement) versus 13%.

The effects of NHI alone on the AFDC program indicate a 2% decline in AFDC caseloads and a 0.4% increase in benefit payments, which appears puzzling (see Table 5-2, cols. 1 & 2). Income counts for AFDC eligibility do not include the in-kind benefit such as health care benefits. Thus, NHI itself should have no effect on AFDC participation. As mentioned in chapter 4, however, it is assumed that employers would increase wage rates in place of current employer contribution to premiums. The 2% decline in AFDC caseloads under NHI comes from taking the post increased earnings into account for AFDC eligibility. Second, the 0.4% increase in benefit payments is related to changes in labor supply in response to NHI. I will discuss more details of labor supply responses to NHI later. In short, the AFDC parents are predicted to decrease hours of work under NHI. Because post AFDC benefits are determined on the basis of post earnings, AFDC benefit amounts are predicted to increase as a result of decreased earnings among the AFDC group. However, it should be emphasized that the magnitude of increase in benefit payments is negligible in the aggregate term.

If the three programs are implemented together, the new regime including CSAS of $2000, children's allowance of $1000, and NHI is predicted to decrease AFDC cases by 21% and AFDC expenditures by 40.2% when current child support payments are assumed. Under the more realistic assumption of medium improvement in child support, more than one-third would leave the AFDC rolls and about 50% of expenditures would be cut down. The much larger impact on AFDC participation under the combined regime is due to the interaction effect of three non-income-tested programs (will be discussed later).

Results for Effects on Food Stamps: Table 5-2 also presents the estimated effects of the reform program(s) on food stamp caseloads and expenditures (see cols. 2 & 3). Families receiving food stamps as of 1988 are estimated at 3.6 million, with total benefits equal to $7.3 billion.

Under CSAS alone, the number of food-stamp families is predicted to decrease by the range of 0.3% to 3.2% depending on assured levels and assumptions of child support. The total expenditure of food stamps would decline by the range of 0.7% to 8.5%. These suggest that CSAS alone would not bring significant savings from food stamps. The predicted effects of children's allowance alone are also not large. Food-stamp families would decline by less than 1% and benefit payments by 5% under the allowance of $409. Even the high level of $1000 allowance is predicted to decrease the number of families only by 4% and expenditures by 14%. The single program of NHI also shows reductions in food stamps, although magnitudes are very small. Similar to the effects of NHI on AFDC, these changes are attributed to changes in post earnings due to conversion of employer-paid premiums and labor supply responses. Changes in the earnings under NHI result in a 1.3% decrease in caseloads and a 0.5% decline in benefit expenditures. Finally, the three-combined reform is estimated to decrease food-stamp cases by about 6% and 9% under pessimistic and optimistic assumptions, respectively. The resulting reduction in the total cost would be in the range of about 18% to 25%, depending on assumptions of child support improvement.

The overall effects of the post program(s) on food stamps are predicted as much less in their magnitudes than those on AFDC. This is because AFDC benefit payments are taken into account in determining food stamp benefits. For example, consider an AFDC family currently receiving the AFDC benefit of $1500 and food stamps of $1000 (based on the AFDC amount of $1500) per year. At the assured benefit of $2000, the family would choose to participate in CSAS and move off AFDC. As a result, the family would be counted as an off-AFDC case and $1500 would be assigned into AFDC savings. Given $2000 from the CSAS program, then, the amount of food stamps would be imputed slightly lower (than the current $1000) due to increased income of $500 (i.e., the difference between the $2000 assured benefit and the $1500 AFDC benefit). The difference of $500 would not be enough for the family to leave the program, and so this family would continue to receive food stamps (but at a slightly lower benefit level) under the reform. This example illustrates why the effects on food stamps are estimated much lower than those on AFDC.

Table 5-2
Effects On Welfare Participation

Pre Reform	AFDC Cases (mill)	AFDC Benefts (bill)	FS Cases (mill)	FS Benefts (bill)	Medcaid Cases (mill)	Medcaid Benefts (bill)
	3.8	$16.1	3.6	$7.3	4.6	$9.9

Post Reform	% Chg in AFDC Cases	% Chg in AFDC Benefts	% Chg in FS Cases	% Chg in FS Benefts	% Chg in Medcaid Cases	% Chg in Medcaid Benefts
CSAS (Under Current Child Support System)						
1000	-0.2	-0.1	-0.3	-0.7	-0.1	-0.1
2000	-1.0	-0.3	-0.7	-1.7	-0.4	-0.2
3000	-3.5	-0.9	-1.5	-3.0	-2.4	-1.4
CSAS (Under Medium Improvement)						
0	-7.5	-13.1	-1.4	-5.2	-5.5	-4.7
1000	-7.9	-13.2	-1.8	-5.9	-5.7	-4.8
2000	-8.4	-13.3	-2.0	-6.8	-6.1	-5.0
3000	-11.2	-13.9	-3.2	-8.5	-8.3	-6.3
Children Allowance						
409	-4.8	-16.8	-0.9	-5.2	-3.7	-4.0
1000	-13.0	-38.7	-4.2	-14.4	-9.9	-10.4
National Health Insurance						
NHI	-2.0	0.4	-1.3	-0.5	-100.0	-100.0
Three Programs Combined: CSAS($2000), CA($1000) & NHI						
Current	-21.0	-40.2	-5.7	-17.6	-100.0	-100.0
Medium	-33.9	-49.8	-8.6	-25.1	-100.0	-100.0

Results for Effects on Medicaid: The final two columns of Table 5-2 show the predicted effects on Medicaid recipiency and expenditures. At the baseline of 1988, the Medicaid program provided health coverage to 4.6 million families and spent $9.9 billion for covered services.

The first two panels of the post reform present the CSAS's effect on the Medicaid program. If medium improvement is achieved in private child support, CSAS alone would bring around a 6-8% reduction in recipient families of Medicaid and around a 5-6% decline in the program cost (see the second panel). In the worst case of no improvement in child support, the range of predicted effects is less than a 2% decrease in Medicaid families and a 1% decrease in expenditures. The children's allowance alone at $409 per child decreases Medicaid recipiency and expenditures by around 4%; and by around 10% at the $1000 allowance. Since Medicaid itself is completely replaced with the system of NHI, percent reductions in Medicaid under the reform involving NHI are all indicated as 100% (see the last two panels of Table 5-2). The resulting public savings from the Medicaid repeal ($9.9 billion) will be taken into account in financing the NHI cost (this will be discussed later in the cost section).

Effects on Income Redistribution

Defining Measures of Income Distribution: Two measures for income distribution are employed. The first measure is the share of income received by each of the five income quintiles. The five income quintiles are arrived at by ranking families according to income, from the poorest to the richest, and then dividing them into five groups, each containing 20% of all families. Total income received by each fifth is expressed as a percentage of total family income.

The second measure is the Gini coefficient, which is affected by changes in all locations in the distribution of income and can be represented with a single summary number. If a family with income above the mean receives $1 less and a family with income below the mean receives an extra $1, then the Gini will fall. On the other hand, if a family with income above the mean receives $1 more and a family with income below the mean receives $1 less, then the Gini will increase. While the Gini coefficient does not have a simple interpretation, it is a widely used summary measure of inequality. The closer it is to one, the more highly are incomes concentrated among a small number of income recipients; the closer it is to zero, the more evenly are incomes distributed across families.

Results for Redistributional Effects: Table 5-3 demonstrates current income distribution and income distribution under the proposed program(s). At the base line of 1988, the poorest fifth of families receives about 6% of total income, while the share of the richest fifth is about 40%, which is almost 7 times as large as the share of the bottom group (see pre-reform panel). Table 5-3 also demonstrates that the share of the top 20% of all families is still larger than that of the bottom three quintiles (sum of shares in 1st, 2nd, and 3rd quintiles is 35.5%).

The second measure of inequality is the Gini coefficient of .343 under the income distribution in 1988 (see Table 5-3, last column of pre-reform). According to Jenkins (1991), a Gini coefficient of .343 can be interpreted to imply that the expected difference in family income between any two families drawn at random from this the income distribution is 34.3%. The estimate of .343 is lower than the .395 estimated by Danziger and Weinberg (1992) as of 1988. The difference might be attributed to different income definitions. This study includes cash values of food stamps, Medicaid, and employer-provided health insurance as well as cash public transfers, while Danziger and Weinberg included only cash transfers from the government. Moreover, not only are earned income tax credits included, but income and payroll taxes are also subtracted in my estimate. On the other hand, neither taxes nor credits are considered in the estimate by Danziger and Weinberg (1991). Adding food stamps, Medicaid, and earned credits as well as subtracting income taxes would particularly contribute to a lower estimate of Gini coefficient than that of Danziger and Weinberg (1991). In addition, defined samples are different: my sample is families with children, while Danziger and Weinberg include all households in their sample. Inclusion of elderly households would contribute to their larger estimate of the Gini coefficient.

Table 5-3
Effects On Income Redistribution

Pre Reform	Percent Distribution of Aggregate Income					Gini Coeff-icient
	Lowest Fifth	2nd Fifth	3rd Fifth	4th Fifth	Highest Fifth	
	5.98	11.83	17.70	24.71	39.78	.343
Post Reform	Lowest Fifth	2nd Fifth	3rd Fifth	4th Fifth	Highest Fifth	Gini
CSAS (Under Current Child Support System)						
1000	6.00	11.83	17.71	24.71	39.75	.342
2000	6.03	11.87	17.72	24.66	39.72	.341
3000	6.09	11.91	17.72	24.64	39.65	.340
CSAS (Under Medium Improvement)						
0	6.16	12.02	17.76	24.62	39.45	.337
1000	6.17	12.03	17.76	24.61	39.43	.337
2000	6.22	12.03	17.77	24.58	39.41	.336
3000	6.28	12.08	17.74	24.57	39.32	.335
Children Allowance						
409	6.13	11.92	17.77	24.61	39.57	.339
1000	6.34	12.09	17.80	24.55	39.21	.333
National Health Insurance						
NHI	6.65	12.48	17.98	24.49	38.41	.322
Three Programs Combined: CSAS($2000), CA($1000) & NHI						
Current	7.12	12.84	18.05	24.22	37.78	.310
Medium	7.37	13.01	18.07	24.09	37.47	.304

Under CSAS alone, shares of the bottom two quintiles increase, those of the top two quintiles slightly decrease, and the middle quintile increases its share but almost unchanged (see Table 5-3, panels 1 & 2 of post reform). Overall magnitudes of impact on income redistribution under the CSAS alone are not large. At most ($3000 plan with medium improvement), the poorest quintile would increase its share by .3 percentage points (from 5.98% to 6.28%); and the share of the second poorest quintile would also increase by almost the same degree (.25 percentage points). Gini coefficients indicate only a small decline in inequality by .008 points (from .343 to .333), even under the $3000 assured level with medium improvement. Moreover, if the more pessimistic assumption is used, the predicted effects of CSAS alone on income inequality are almost negligible.

It should be noted that CSAS involves income redistribution through two ways: (a) CSAS redistributes incomes from the public to custodial parents in the form of assured benefits; and (b) CSAS redistributes incomes from noncustodial parents to custodial parents in the form of private child support. However, this study only takes into account income changes of custodial parents and ignores changes in incomes of noncustodial parents. Since noncustodial parents typically have higher incomes than custodial parents, my estimated effect of CSAS on income redistribution is downward biased. Put another way, CSAS might have somewhat larger redistributional effects if noncustodial parents' income losses were taken into account in income distribution.

The single program of children's allowance is predicted to have slightly larger effects on income redistribution than CSAS alone does (see Table 5-3, panel 3 of post reform). This is because the children's allowance benefits more families, compared with the CSAS being limited to custodial families with awards. As shown in Table 5-3, the children's allowance of $409 would increase income shares by .15 percentage points (from 5.98% to 6.13%) for the lowest quintile. The $1000 allowance benefit families at the bottom more: it would increase their income shares to 6.34 (a .36 percentage points increase). The inequality is estimated to decrease from .343 to .339 due to the allowance level of $409; and to .333 due to the $1000 level.

The NHI is predicted as more effective for income redistribution than any other single program, although payroll taxes imply a regressive financing tool (see Table 5-3, panel 4 of post reform). It would increase the income share of the bottom group by .67

percentage points, compared to .3 percentage points (under CSAS of $3000 with medium improvement) and .36 percentage points (under children's allowance of $1000). For the second bottom quintile, the share would be increased by .65 percentage points under NHI, compared with .25 percentage points under the $3000 CSAS with medium improvement and .26 percentage points under the $1000 children allowance. On the other hand, the top group would lose income most under NHI. The income share of the top quintile would decline by about 1.4 percentage points (from 39.8% to 38.4%) due to NHI, compared to a .5 percentage points decrease due to CSAS of $3000 (medium) and a .6 percentage points decrease due to the children's allowance of $1000. Accordingly, NHI would reduce inequality from .343 to .322. This Gini is compared with .335 (under the $3000 CSAS with medium) and .333 (under the $1000 allowance).

        The three-combined reform is predicted to smooth current income skewness significantly (see Table 5-3, the last panel). Using the medium assumption, the share of the poorest group is estimated to raise from 5.98% to 7.37% (1.4 percentage points increase); and the share of the second poorest group would increase from 11.8 to 13% (1.2 percentage points increase). In contrast, the top richest group would lose 2.3% of its original income share; and the fourth fifth would decrease its share by .6 percentage points. The middle income group (the third fifth) would benefit slightly by increasing its share by .4 percentage points. The estimated Gini coefficient under the same assumption reaches to .304 (from .343). The no improvement assumption in child support pushes down the magnitudes of effects of the combined regime on income redistribution. However, estimates are not far away from those under the medium assumption. The more significant effects under the combined regime appear to come from some interaction effects when the programs are implemented together.

Effects on Labor Supply

The predicted changes in the mean hours worked of parents are presented in Table 5-4, separately for those originally receiving AFDC and for those not on AFDC. Before the reform, the mean hours annually worked is 264 hours for AFDC recipients, and 1,523 hours for non-AFDC parents. The overall mean hours of all parents is 1,439 hours during the year 1988. The mean hours of AFDC parents is low because many AFDC parents are nonworkers or part-time workers.

Table 5-4
Labor Supply Response: Mean Hours Worked

Pre Reform	Among People Originally on AFDC		Among People Originally not on AFDC		All People	
Ave Hrs	264		1523		1439	
Post Reform	Among AFDC		Among non-AFDC		Among All	
	Ave Hrs	% Chg	Ave Hrs	% Chg	Ave Hrs	% Chg
CSAS (Under Current Child Support System)						
1000	266	.6	1522	-.0	1438	-.0
2000	269	1.7	1521	-.1	1437	-.1
3000	274	3.6	1519	-.3	1436	-.2
CSAS (Under Medium Improvement)						
0	275	3.9	1514	-.6	1431	-.5
1000	277	5.0	1514	-.6	1431	-.5
2000	280	6.1	1514	-.6	1431	-.5
3000	286	8.3	1513	-.6	1431	-.5
Children Allowance						
409	266	.7	1516	-.5	1432	-.4
1000	274	3.8	1498	-1.6	1416	-1.6
National Health Insurance						
NHI	259	-1.8	1503	-1.3	1420	-1.3
Three Programs Combined: CSAS($2000), CA($1000) & NHI						
Current	292	10.7	1481	-2.7	1402	-2.6
Medium	312	18.3	1474	-3.2	1397	-2.9

Under the post-reform, as indicated under no improvement in child support, CSAS of $2000 assured benefit would slightly increase the annual mean hours by 5 hours (1.7% increase) among parents originally receiving AFDC; the mean hours would further go up by 10 hours (3.6% increase) under $3000 assurance with current child support (see Table 5-4, panel 1 of post reform, cols. 1 & 2). Among non-AFDC parents using the same assumption of current child support, on the other hand, the mean hours are estimated to slightly decrease by 2 hours (0.1% decline) at the $2000 assured level and 4 hours (0.3% decrease) at the $3000 level (see cols. 3 & 4). On net among all parents, the mean hours decrease by 2 hours (0.1% decline) at the $2000 assured level and 3 hours (0.2% decline) at the $3000 level under the current child support assumption (see cols. 5 & 6).

As mentioned earlier, CSAS itself is expected to increase private child support. If the percentage standard is adopted for establishing award levels, and award and collection rates are increased by half the distance from the current to the perfect system, the effects of increased private child support on labor supply are as follows: mean hours would increase by 11 hours (3.9% increase) among AFDC custodial parents; mean hours would decrease by 9 hours (0.6% decline) among non-AFDC parents; and this would result in a net decrease of 8 hours annually (0.5% decline) among all parents (see the first row of panel 2 in post reform).

If we consider both medium-increased child support and assured benefits together, magnitudes of labor responses to CSAS are predicted slightly larger than when only increased child support is considered. Among AFDC parents, the mean hours would increase by 16 hours (6.1% increase) at the $2000 assured benefit and 22 hours (8.3% increase) at the $3000 benefit. Among non-AFDC parents, the decrease of mean hours would be 9 hours (0.6% decline) and 10 hours (0.6% decline) at $2000 and $3000 assured levels, respectively. The overall change including all custodial parents under CSAS is predicted at a decrease of 8 hours (0.5% decline) per year, but this is almost insensitive to levels of assured benefits (see final column, panel 2 of post reform).[2]

In brief, as expected, the labor supply response to increased private child support and assured benefits is an increase among parents on AFDC, but a decrease among non-AFDC parents. Because AFDC parents are a small proportion of the population and their base-line hours of work are relatively low, their increased hours do not outweigh the decreased hours among non-AFDC parents, resulting in an overall decline in the aggregate. However, the net decline in the mean hours of work due to CSAS is not substantial--less than 8 hours per year (0.5% decline). Second, the positive labor supply responses of AFDC parents get larger as the assured benefit level increases. By contrast, the negative responses of parents not on AFDC is insensitive to the level of assured benefit.

The third panel of the post reform in Table 5-4 presents the labor supply effects of the children's allowance alone. The low level of allowance ($409 per child) would increase the annual amount of work by 2 hours (0.7% increase) on average for parents on AFDC; would decrease by 7 hours (0.5% decline) for those not on AFDC; and would result in the netting-out decrease of 7 hours (0.4% decline) for all parents, all indicating marginal effects. Unlike CSAS, labor supply responses appear to be sensitive to the level of children's allowance. Under the high level of $1000 allowance, labor supply responses become larger in their magnitudes. In response to the $1000 plan per child, the annual hours of work on average would increase by 10 hours (3.8% increase) among AFDC parents; decrease by 25 hours (1.6%) among non-AFDC parents; and the overall change would be a decrease of 23 hours (1.6% decline) for all parents per year. The twenty-three hour decline on net under the $1000 allowance is compared with only 7 hours decline due to the $409 plan. The overall negative effect of the $1000 allowance on the labor supply is larger than any other single program.

The single program of NHI is predicted identically to decrease hours of work for all groups (see panel 4 of post reform). NHI would decrease the annual labor supply by 5 hours (1.8% decline) on average among AFDC parents; 20 hours (1.3% decline) among the non-AFDC group; and 19 hours (1.3% decline) among the whole group of parents. Under NHI, the estimated negative effect on labor supply for the AFDC group appears puzzling. Theoretically, AFDC recipients are likely to work more under the NHI program, because the disincentives of Medicaid to work no longer exist. On the other hand, NHI provides more unearned income than current Medicaid. The mean of NHI values is $2821, whereas Medicaid values are averaged at $2110. Some AFDC mothers particularly residing in those states which provide much lower values of Medicaid would face substantial increases in unearned income in the form of health care benefits. Since the model of labor supply simulation includes the cash values of health care benefits, this increased unearned income would have an income effect which leads those to work less. In addition, the NHI program requires higher taxes for working AFDC recipients in two ways: higher income taxes due to a conversion of employer-paid premiums into increased earnings if the recipient is currently covered through employer insurance; and higher payroll taxes of 7.1% on earned incomes (note that the proposed NHI does not exempt payroll taxes for the poor). These increased taxes required under NHI would have two opposite effects: the income effect (work more) and the substitution effect (work less). However, the net effect from all positive and negative forces on the labor supply among AFDC working mothers is empirically uncertain. The estimated decrease of 5 hours on average among AFDC parents in this study indicates that negative effects (work less) outweigh positive effects (work more) on their labor supply. This also causes the prediction that AFDC benefit payments would increase by 0.4% under NHI (Table 5-2), because, as discussed earlier, post AFDC benefits are determined according to post decreased earnings. However, it should be emphasized that the negative effect of NHI on the labor supply response of AFDC mothers is not large in the aggregate term.

When the three programs are implemented together, labor supply responses among AFDC parents are predicted to substantially increase (see Table 5-4, cols. 1 & 2, final panel). Parents on AFDC increase their mean hours by 48 hours (18.3% increase) under the medium assumption and by 28 hours (10.7% increase) under the current child support assumption. On the other hand, labor supply responses among non-AFDC parents are predicted to somewhat decrease: by 49 hours (3.2% decline) and 42 hours (2.7% decline) per year under the medium and no improvement assumptions in child support, respectively. The overall decrease for all parents would be in the range between 37 hours (2.6% decline under no improvement scenario) and 42 hours (2.9% decline under medium scenario).

Generally, the results correspond to a theoretical expectation of labor supply behaviors. Individuals on AFDC tend to increase work in response to non-income-tested transfers. However, the reverse holds for non-AFDC individuals: they as a group tend to decrease hours of work. Although the positive effects of the AFDC group are larger than the negative effects of the non-AFDC group, the overall change in the labor supply is negative. This is because AFDC recipients are a relatively small number in the population. This supports the general belief that the labor supply would decrease in response to an increase in income guarantee. However, the size of that negative effect is not large, at most a less than 3% decrease even under the benefit package of three programs.

Looking at changes in the mean hours can overlook some information on specific changes in labor supply behaviors, because the mean hours are generated by averaging out different work behavior patterns. An important policy question is how many non-working AFDC parents would begin to work in response to policy changes (Table 5-4 does not present this information). Under single programs, the percentages of non-workers on AFDC who go to work are predicted to be relatively small. The CSAS of $2000 under medium improvement is predicted to enable 1.2% of non-workers on AFDC to start work, with hours worked predicted at 250 hours on average per year; and CSAS of $3000 would bring 2% of AFDC non-workers to begin to work at annual hours of 248 on average. Under the single programs of children's allowance and NHI, the percentage of non-workers on AFDC who go to work would be less than 1%. However, the combined regime encourages a significant percentage of AFDC non-workers to participate in the work force. Under the medium assumption, the combined package of $2000 CSAS, $1000 children's allowance, and NHI would bring more than 10% of AFDC non-workers to work at average hours of 253 per year. This magnitude is much larger than the single program's effects. This larger percentage indicates that the combined benefit package will enable non-working AFDC recipients to work off welfare or to be better off with earnings combined with new program benefits rather than solely depending on AFDC amounts. It is also implied that any single program reform alone is not enough to make AFDC recipients better off with the benefits plus earnings.

Interaction Effects of Three-Combined Programs

One of research questions in this study is to look at interaction effects which would result when the three non-income-tested programs are combined. An interesting pattern is found in the labor supply effects under the combined regime. For parents on AFDC, the positive effects of non-income-tested transfer on their labor supply behaviors appear substantially strengthened when the programs are combined. For parents not on AFDC, by contrast, the negative effects on their labor supply seem somewhat weakened under the combined regime.

If we look at changes in the mean hours in Table 5-5, the number of increased hours for the AFDC group is substantially larger under the combined regime than the sum of increased hours under the single program (see row 2). Among AFDC parents, the mean hours are predicted to increase by 16 hours per year under the CSAS of $2000 assured benefit (medium assumption); increase by 10 hours under the $1000 children's allowance; decrease by 5 hours under NHI. These predicted changes in the mean hours under each of the single programs are summed to the increase of 21 hours. On the other hand, the combined regime (medium) is predicted to increase by 48 hours on average per year. This indicates that the combined regime yields a 27 hour increase over the addition of single programs' mean hours changes--more than twice as many hours. This difference implies that the non-income-tested programs have a strong upward interaction for the positive effects on the labor supply among the AFDC group when they are combined. The work incentive effect for non-working AFDC parents also becomes even more strengthened under the three-combined programs (see Table 5-5, row 1). The predicted percentage of non-workers on AFDC who begin to work is 1.2% under the CSAS of $2000 (medium); 0.9% under the children's allowance of $1000; 0.2% under NHI. These percentages are summed to 2.3%. When these programs are implemented together, 10.3% of non-working AFDC parents are predicted to start work. This percentage is 5 times as large as the sum of single effects, indicating that the combined non-income-tested programs provide spring-board incentives for non-working AFDC parents to work.

The strong upward interaction for the AFDC group brings up an important policy implication. This interaction implies that any single program reform alone is not enough to bring AFDC recipients out of welfare dependency. Only the combined benefit package will enable AFDC recipients to work off welfare or to be better off with earnings combined with public benefits rather than solely depending on AFDC benefits. In terms of public concerns for welfare dependency, in particular, a greater implication can be advanced for parents on AFDC who begin to work under the combined regime. Once they begin to work (even a small number of hours), they are more likely to have job information and a chance at improving job skills. Once connections to the job market are built up, they are more likely to eventually work off welfare. Thus, only a comprehensive reform with the three combined programs will bring welfare dependents to a route of self-sufficiency.

Table 5-5

Comparison Of Combined Effect With Sum Of Single Effects

		Effects of Single Program				Effects of Combined Programs (Medium)
		CSAS ($2000) w/ Medium	Children Allowance ($1000)	NHI	Sum	
AFDC [a] Group	% [d] Begn	+1.2	+0.9	+0.2	+2.3	+10.3
	Chg [e] Hrs	+16	+10	-5	+21	+48
Non [b] AFDC	Chg [e] Hrs	-9	-25	-20	-54	-49
All [c]	Chg [e] Hrs	-8	-23	-19	-50	-42
% Chg in AFDC Case		-8.4	-13.0	-2.0	-23.4	-33.9
% Chg in FS Case		-2.0	-4.2	-1.3	-7.5	-8.6
% Chg in Pov Rate		-8.0	-15.3	-22.6	-45.9	-50.6
% Chg in Pov Gap		-9.0	-21.6	-32.3	-62.9	-61.4

Notes:
[a] Parents originally on AFDC;
[b] Parents not on AFDC;
[c] Including AFDC and non-AFDC parents;
[d] Percent of non-workers on AFDC who begin to work;
[e] Changes in the mean hours.

For the non-AFDC group, a downward interaction in the mean hours is found, but its magnitude is rather small. As seen in Table 5-5 (row 3), all sets of simulation are predicted to have negative effects on the mean hours for the non-AFDC group. Among non-AFDC parents, the sum of the single programs' effects is a decrease of 54 hours (-9 - 25 -20). On the other hand, the combined regime is estimated to decrease the mean hours by 49 hours. This magnitude is 5 hours less than the addition of single effects, indicating a small downward interaction for the negative effects on the labor supply among non-AFDC parents. For the whole group (including all parents), the downward interaction in the mean hours increases. The combined regime decreases 42 hours on average per year (see Table 5-5, row 4). This decrease of 42 hours is compared with the 50 hours from the addition of decreased mean hours of each single program, indicating that the overall negative effects are weakened by 16%. The downward interaction for overall negative labor supply responses among all parents brings up another important implication for policy makers. Generally, it is believed that a universal income guarantee would result in a significant efficiency loss as a whole. It is expected that the higher income guarantee is introduced, the more loss of efficiency would be resulted. Research evidence in this study supports that negative effects exist due to a universal income guarantee, as expected. However, this study finds that the negative effects for the whole group under the three-combined regime are 84% in magnitude than the addition of single programs' effects. This implies that a universal income guarantee would not result in a efficiency loss as proportionately as the level of guarantee increases.

Interaction effects are also found, particularly in welfare participation and poverty measures. The sum of the single programs' effects on reduction of AFDC caseloads reveals a 23.4% decline using the medium scenario of CSAS (see Table 5-5, row 5). This sum is lower than the 34% decrease in AFDC caseloads under the combined regime. This comparison indicates that when the three programs are combined, the impact on AFDC reduction becomes substantially strengthened (achieving a 10 percentage points greater) due to the interaction of programs. Similarly, the combined effect on food stamp participation is estimated at a 8.6% decrease which is larger than the sum of single programs' effects (7.5%).

The same pattern is found for the combined effects on the poverty rate. The percent reductions in the poverty rate due to each single program are summed to 45.9% under medium improvement. Again, the combined effects are greater than the simple sum of the single programs' effects: about a 5 percentage points greater (50.6% combined vs. 45.9% summed). It again appears that the three non-income-tested programs, when they are combined, produce upward-interaction effects which make the combined regime more effective as an anti-poverty tool to reduce the number of poor families. However, the magnitude of the upward-interaction effect on poverty is smaller than that on AFDC participation.

On the other hand, the combined programs produce a small negative interaction for the effect on the poverty gap (see final row, Table 5-5). The combined effect on the poverty gap is a decrease of 61.4%, which is slightly less than the sum of the single programs' effects (a decrease of 62.9%), indicating the negative interaction under the combined programs. Given that the combined effect on reduction in the poverty rate is predicted larger than the sum of the single programs' effects, this negative interaction for the poverty gap appears puzzling. However, some families with incomes slightly below the poverty threshold contribute to this negative interaction. Take the following case, where the pre-income level is $11,000 and the poverty line is $12,000, as an example. Suppose that CSAS alone increases the family's income to $13,000; children's allowance alone increases the income level to $12,000; and the single program of NHI increases the income to $14,000. Under these three single programs, the sum of reductions in the poverty gap is $3,000 ($1,000 under each single program). Under the three-combined programs, the family's income would increase to the much higher income level of $16,000, but the amount of poverty gap reduced would remain the same as that of a single program ($1,000). In other words, families with incomes slightly off the poverty threshold are easily taken out of poverty by a single program. With the combined benefit package, not only are these families always taken out of poverty, but also the amount of poverty gap reduced under the combined programs is always less than the sum of the poverty gap reduced under each single program. This example helps to explain why the positive interaction for the poverty rate and the negative interaction for the poverty gap both exist.

Components of Cost and Savings, and Net Costs

Table 5-6 shows the components of costs and savings associated with the proposed program(s). The first column presents the estimated gross cost of the program(s); columns 2 through 4 show the components of welfare savings resulting from the non-income-tested program(s); column 5 includes changes in earned income tax credit (EITC) due to changes in earnings under reform(s); column 6 includes income tax changes (due to labor supply changes) as well as income tax revenues (collected from raising tax rates); column 7 shows income tax revenues from taxing the public portions of assured benefits and children's allowances; the payroll tax revenues of column 8 are associated with a payroll tax rate of 7.1% for financing NHI cost; and, for the final column, net costs are derived by taking into account all the components of cost and savings presented in the previous columns.

Child Support Assurance Alone: The gross cost for CSAS is estimated at the range of $491 million to $7.4 billion in 1988 figures, depending on assured levels and child support assumptions. The estimated gross cost for CSAS are higher under the no improvement assumption than under medium improvement, because the public cost of assured benefit received by a family is determined by private child support paid. Also, the total cost of the CSAS program increases as the assured benefit increases because of providing higher income guarantees. The CSAS of $1000 is estimated to require a gross cost of $1 billion under no improvement and $491 million under medium improvement in child support. For the CSAS of $2000, the gross cost is estimated at $3.4 billion and $2.2 billion under no improvement and under medium improvement, respectively. The CSAS of $3000 would require a gross cost from $5.3 billion (under medium) to $7.4 billion (under current).

    The resulting AFDC savings from the CSAS implementation are as follows (see Table 5-6, col. 2, panels 1 & 2). The estimated dollar amounts of AFDC savings are small when current child support is assumed (at most, $138 million at the $3000 level). However, the medium improvement scenario indicates an AFDC savings of more than $2 billion at all levels of assured benefit. The increased award levels and child support collections play a major role in bringing these AFDC savings. At the assured benefit of $0 under medium improvement, the increased child support already achieves a savings of $2.1 billion.

Reading down the panel of medium scenario, the estimated amount of AFDC savings slightly increases, but remains fairly constant as the level of assurance increases (see Table 5-6, col. 2, panel 2). The dollar amounts of savings from food stamps are estimated as much less than those from AFDC (see col. 3). The estimated savings from food stamps are in the range of $51 million to $624 million, depending on assured levels and child support assumptions. For example, CSAS of $2000 would result in a savings of $128 million under no improvement and $501 million under medium improvement. Another component of welfare savings is from Medicaid (see col. 4). The Medicaid savings are closely associated with AFDC exits. Estimated savings are $22 million under the $2000 assured level with current child supports and about $497 million under the $2000 level with medium improvement.

Estimated changes in earned income tax credits (EITC) indicate an increase in EITC costs due to the CSAS program (see Table 5-6, col. 5). EITC participation is expected to increase because some non-workers on AFDC begin to work. Amounts of credit are also likely to increase because some AFDC working mothers increase their hours and earn more, and because some non-AFDC custodial parents, decreasing their work hours as unearned income increases, fall into incomes below the threshold of EITC eligibility. However, estimated costs of EITC due to these work responses are not large--$101 million at most. At the $2000 assured benefit, for example, EITC costs would increase by $14 million under no improvement and $77 million under the medium improvement scenario. As also seen in the table, EITC costs increase as assured levels increase because magnitudes of work response get bigger.

Income taxes are predicted to decrease due to CSAS implementation, because overall hours worked decrease on average (see Table 5-6, col. 6). As previously discussed in the labor supply effects, increased child support for upper-income custodial parents decreases their labor supply and thus decreases their tax liability as well, which outweighs any increased taxes paid from those who earn more. The loss of income tax revenue at the $2000 CSAS is estimated at $90 million under current child support and $838 million under medium improvement. Income tax revenues from taxing public portions of assured benefit are presented in column 7. At the $2000 assured benefit, additional income taxes collected as a take-back of public assured benefits are estimated at $448 million under no improvement and $278 million under medium improvement. The higher income tax collections under no improvement than under medium improvement are primarily because of a greater decrease in labor supply due to increased child supports under medium improvement. As also shown in column 7, more taxes (from assured benefits) are collected as an assured level increases.

Net costs for the CSAS single program are derived by combining all components of cost and savings presented in the previous columns (see Table 5-6, col. 9): positive signs indicate a net cost and negative signs indicate a net savings. For a net cost of CSAS alone, components of savings include those from AFDC, food stamps, and Medicaid, and additional income tax revenue from assured benefits; cost components include an additional cost for EITC and a loss of income tax revenues due to labor supply changes. The estimated net costs indicate that the CSAS program alone would not be costly, and might even bring some savings. If medium improvement is achieved in private child support, CSAS with no assured benefit would save $2.1 billion. This savings would reduce to $1.7 billion under the CSAS with the $1000 assured benefit, and to $358 million under the plan of $2000. However, the highest level of $3000 becomes a cost-incurring plan; this plan could be instituted at a cost of $2.1 billion. If current child support continues, CSAS is predicted to require some cost: a net cost of $0.9 billion to $6.3 billion for the three different levels of assured benefit.

Children's Allowance Alone: The third panel of Table 5-6 presents the components of cost and savings for the plans of children's allowance. The children's allowance of $409 per child is estimated at a gross cost of $27.8 billion. The plan of $409 would result in a savings of $2.7 billion from the AFDC program, $385 million from food stamps, and $398 million from Medicaid (see cols. 2, 3 & 4). This plan also would take back $4.6 billion through income taxes by taxing allowances (see col. 7). However, the plan would result in a greater cost for EITC due to work responses, which is estimated at $31 million (see col. 5). Counted together, the remaining cost for the allowance plan of $409 is $19.7 billion. This cost is financed through income tax revenues from repealing tax exemptions for children. The tax revenue of $19.7 billion (in col. 6) is obtained after the decline in income tax liabilities due to labor supply responses is taken into account. Because the level of allowance is determined so that the plan is cost-neutral, the estimated net cost is presented at zero (see col. 7).

The children's allowance of $1000 per child is predicted to require a much higher gross cost--about $68 billion. This total cost would go down to about $59.7 by taking out the savings from welfare programs--about $6.3 billion from AFDC (col. 2), about $1.1 billion from food stamps (col. 3), and $1 billion from Medicaid (col. 4). Again, treating allowances as taxable income would create a tax revenue of $13 billion (col. 7), making the cost decrease to $46.5 billion. As explained before, EITC would cost more due to labor supply changes, estimated at $206 million (col. 5). If this EITC cost is included, the total cost then increases to $46.7 billion. To finance this cost of $46.7 billion, a 2.7% increase in income tax rates as well as the elimination of exemptions for children are assumed. The tax revenue associated with exemptions for children is estimated at about $20 billion; and the revenue collected from families with children under the increased income tax rates is estimated at about $7 billion. Put together, the total revenue of additional income taxes collected from families with children is $27 billion. However, increased tax rates should be applied to all households, including the elderly and single individuals. As mentioned in the methods section of chapter 4, the income tax revenue collected from households other than families with children is $19.5 billion.[3] Thus, the total income tax revenue arrived at is $46.7 billion (see col. 6). With this revenue taken into account, the result is a net cost of zero (col. 9).

National Health Insurance Alone: NHI (mean cash value of $2821 per family) is estimated to require a gross cost of more than $104 billion. A few things should be noted in this estimate of gross cost. First, the estimated cost of $104 billion is to cover all children under age 18 and their parents. The nonelderly individuals without children and the elderly are not included in this cost estimate. Second, no increase in health care utilization is considered. The level of utilization would be affected by the benefit package and the structure of cost sharing such as a rate of coinsurance or a copayment. NHI is proposed to provide the same benefit package as the average level of current employer-provided insurance, and requires the same rate of coinsurance. Thus, individuals covered currently through employer-related insurance or Medicaid would not significantly increase health utilization. However, currently uninsured individuals (14.7% of the sample persons) would increase utilization responding to first-dollar coverage, which implies that the estimate of $104 billion might be understated. The gross cost of NHI for currently uninsured children and parents (in the sample) amounts to $12.6 billion. Assuming a 23% increase in health care spending for this group,[4] for example, the cost would increase to $15.5 billion, indicating an underestimate of $2.9 billion due to ignoring the utilization change of the uninsured group. In addition, currently under-insured individuals might increase utilization, but predicting the extent of such a change is difficult. Third, administrative savings associated with a single payer system of NHI are not considered, and thus contribute to over-estimating the cost. Zedlewski et al. (1993) employed 5% as an administrative load factor under a single payer system with cost sharing, while under the current employer-based insurance they reported 26% for the firm size having 10-499 employees and 9% for firms employing more than 500.[5] Taking the difference between 26% and 5% implies an overestimate of $21.8 billion (.21*104 billion). Taking the difference between 9% and 5%, the overestimated cost from ignoring administrative loads would be $4.2 billion. Since the administrative savings seem larger than the cost increase due to utilization changes, the estimate of $104 for a NHI gross cost may provide the upper limit. Since there would be many uncertain changes from NHI implementation, the seemingly over-estimated total cost is adopted without a downward adjustment. At the least, the over-estimated gross cost provides a more conservative estimation.

Under NHI, a major savings comes from current Medicaid expenditures (about $9.9 billion as of 1988), because of integrating the program into the NHI system (see Table 5-6, col. 4).[6] Although values of health care benefits have nothing to do with benefit calculation of AFDC, the cost of $58 million (see col. 2) indicates that AFDC benefit payments increase under the NHI program. This puzzling prediction is related again to labor supply responses (work less) among AFDC parents under the NHI program (see previous discussion in section D in this chapter). NHI is predicted to save food stamp expenditures ($39 million), which is also attributed to labor supply changes (see Table 5-6, col. 3). In addition, NHI is predicted to bring in more income tax revenue--$11.8 billion (col. 6). This tax revenue is generated because current employer-paid premiums (tax exempted) are converted into increased earnings under NHI. This estimated tax revenue ($11.8 billion) is obtained after labor supply responses are taken into account. Since earnings change (due to labor supply changes as well as increased earnings from current employer-paid premiums) under NHI, earned income tax credits also change. NHI is predicted to decrease tax credits, resulting in EITC savings of $492 billion (col. 5). The predicted savings from EITC appears related to decreases in hours worked by low-income individuals in response to higher taxes required for the NHI financing. If we carry all these components of cost and savings into the estimated gross cost of NHI, the remaining cost becomes $81.96 billion. To finance this cost, the payroll tax rate of 7.1% is imposed, which is estimated to result in about $81.96 billion. With this revenue from payroll taxes, the result is a net cost of zero.

Regarding the results for NHI, it should be mentioned that the NHI simulation in this study differs in program features from the Clinton administration's health plan. While President Clinton has proposed an employer mandate with multiple insurers, this study simulates a sole insurer by the government. Also, while the Clinton's proposal involves shifting program costs to employers, this study employs a self-financing scheme through payroll taxes. Therefore, my results cannot provide answers about the possible impacts of the administration's health plan, particularly for the question of who bears what cost. However, my results bring some implications for the administration's plan. First, my estimate for the total gross cost of NHI for families with children ($104 billion) would be approximately close to the total cost required for these families under Clinton's plan, particularly because this study ignores an increase in utilization and an administrative savings due to the single payer system.[7] Second, in this study, the current employers' premium contribution to cover employees with children and their dependents is estimated at $65 billion. Also, the total Medicaid cost for families with children is estimated at about $10 billion. These estimates imply that employers hiring parents with children would have to pay an additional cost of $29 billion (that is, $104 billion - $65 billion - $10 billion) if Clinton's health plan were implemented. Third, this study examines the antipoverty and redistributional effects of the benefit structure under NHI. If we ignore a difference in the financing structure between two proposals, the estimated effects of NHI through the benefit structure on poverty and income distribution in this study could be generalized for Clinton's health plan.

Three Programs Combined: Under the non-income-tested regime of three programs combined, the estimated costs and savings are as follows (see Table 5-6, final panel). The gross costs for each separate element of the post regime are: from $3.2 billion to $4.2 billion for CSAS of $2000 under no improvement and medium improvement in child support, respectively; $68 billion for the children's allowance of $1000; and $104 billion for NHI. Gross costs for CSAS under the combined regime are estimated higher than those under the single program: for $2000 CSAS with the no improvement scenario, the gross cost of $4.2 billion estimated under the combined regime is higher than the $3.4 billion under the single program of CSAS; and with medium improvement, $3.2 billion (estimated under the combined regime) is larger than $2.2 billion (estimated under single CSAS). These higher estimates of gross cost are related to AFDC participation. The combined regime (providing larger benefits) enables more AFDC cases to exit the program and participate in CSAS, compared to the single CSAS. This results in more AFDC savings and higher costs for CSAS under the combined regime. For the three programs combined, the total gross cost is estimated in the range of $175.3 billion (medium scenario) to $176.3 billion (no improvement scenario).[8]

The combined regime under the no improvement scenario would generate welfare savings of $17.6 billion in total: $6.5 billion from AFDC; $1.3 billion from food stamps; and $9.9 billion from Medicaid. Under the medium scenario, a total of $19.7 billion would be saved in welfare expenditures: $8.0 billion from AFDC; $1.8 billion from food stamps; and $9.9 billion from Medicaid. Also, EITC costs are predicted to decrease because of labor supply responses to combined benefits, resulting in a savings of $180 million (under medium scenario) to $281 million (under current scenario) (see col. 5). The income tax revenue (col. 6) includes additional tax collections from raising tax rates (2.7% increase), eliminating exemptions for children, and converting current employer contributions into increased earnings. In addition, tax revenue incorporates changes in labor supply. The estimated revenue from these income taxes is between $40 billion (medium scenario) and $41 billion (current scenario). Including income taxes collected from households other than families with children ($19.5 billion), the total income tax revenue reaches the range of $59.7 billion (medium) to $60.7 billion (current) (see col. 6). Taxation on children's allowances and assured benefits would also generate an additional revenue of around $14 billion (see col. 7). The estimated revenue from payroll taxes (7.1%) for financing NHI cost would be $81 billion (see col. 8), which is slightly lower than the estimate under the single NHI program due to labor supply changes. Counted together, a net cost is estimated in the range between $2.6 billion (under current scenario) and $1 billion (under medium scenario). Since no financing schedule is set up for CSAS, this net cost results from implementing the CSAS of $2000 assured benefit. The CSAS net cost of $2.6 billion estimated under the combined regime with the current child support assumption is slightly lower than that estimated under the single CSAS ($2.9 billion). On the other hand, the estimated net cost of $1 billion for CSAS under the combined regime (medium improvement) is higher than that under the single CSAS (a savings of $358 million). It should be remembered that the gross cost of the CSAS component increases by $1 billion when the $2000 CSAS is combined with the children's allowance and NHI, because more AFDC cases participate in CSAS under the combined regime. At the same time, off-AFDC cases bring more AFDC savings under the combined regime. An increased net cost for CSAS under the combined run means that the increased gross cost for CSAS may not be offset by AFDC savings.

Table 5-6

Components Of Costs And Savings Under Reform

Post Reform	Total Cost (1)	AFDC Sav (2)	FS Sav (3)	Medcaid Sav (4)	EITC Chg (5)	Inc Tax Chg (6)	Inc Tax (Ben) (7)	Payroll Tax (8)	Net Cost (9)
CSAS (Under Current Child Support System): $ millions									
1000	1,048	19	51	5	1	-52	118	-	908
2000	3,432	51	128	22	14	-90	448	-	2,889
3000	7,442	138	219	137	49	-304	989	-	6,312
CSAS (Under Medium Improvement): $ millions									
0	0	2,119	380	461	75	-805	0	-	-2,080
1000	491	2,131	433	477	71	-806	53	-	-1,727
2000	2,153	2,150	501	497	77	-838	278	-	-358
3000	5,259	2,246	624	619	101	-896	656	-	2,111

Table 5-6 continues

Post Reform	Total Cost (1)	AFDC Sav (2)	FS Sav (3)	Medcaid Sav (4)	EITC Chg (5)	Inc Tax Chg (6)	Inc Tax (Ben) (7)	Payroll Tax (8)	Net Cost (9)
Children Allowance: $ millions									
409	27,785	2,716	385	398	31	19,666	4,648	-	0
1000	67,988	6,250	1,058	1,025	206	46,704	13,157	-	0
National Health Insurance: $ millions									
NHI	104,121	-58	39	9,853	-492	11,835	-	81,959	0
Three Programs Combined: CSAS($2000), CA($1000) & NHI: $ millions									
Current	176,317 CSAS=4,208 CA=67,988 NHI=104,121	6,481	1,295	9,853	-281	60,693	14,051	81,113	2,550
Medium	175,305 CSAS=3,196 CA=67,988 NHI=104,121	8,040	1,841	9,853	-180	59,727	13,815	80,847	1,002

Table 5-6 continues

Notes:

(5) Post total amount of EITC - Pre total amount of EITC. The minus sign indicates a savings and the plus sign indicates a cost.

(6) Post total income taxes - Pre total income taxes, due to labor supply changes. For simulation with CA of $409, this includes the income tax revenue associated with eliminating exemptions for children, and for CA of $1000, the tax revenue from increasing the tax rate by 2.7% is additionally included. The income tax revenue collected from households other than families with children ($19.5 billion) is counted in the table where CA of $1000 is involved. For simulation involving NHI, this includes the tax revenue from eliminating exemptions for employer contribution to premium costs.

(7) The total of income taxes collected from taxing public assured benefit and children allowance.

(8) The tax revenue from increasing the payroll tax rate by 7.08% for financing NHI total cost.

(9) Net Cost = - Total Cost + AFDC Savings + Stamps Savings + Medicaid Savings - EITC Change + Income Tax Change + Income Tax on Assured Benefit and CA + Payroll Tax Revenue.

Sensitivity Test to Values of Health Care Coverage

The results presented so far depend on the valuation method of medical care, which is based on the market costs of provision. To test sensitivity to valuation of health care, coverage values are discounted by 58%, which represents the lowest estimate existing for a recipient value. Coverage values include Medicaid, Medicare, employer-provided health insurance, and NHI. Table 5-7 presents the results from these discounted values. To show how the results are sensitive to the recipient's discounted rate, the results from the original market values (un-discounted) are also included in the table.

In simulation for the sensitivity test, the CSAS of $2000 assured benefit with medium improvement in child support, and the children's allowance of $1000 are selected. In these sets of simulation, health care coverage involves Medicaid, Medicare, and employer insurance, each with market values and discounted values, separately. As seen in the first two panels of Table 5-7, discounted values of medical care do not significantly change the estimated effects of the program on the poverty gap, food stamp caseloads, and income distribution measured as a Gini coefficient. However, percent changes in AFDC participation and the mean hours of AFDC parents appear slightly sensitive to discounted values, although the differences are not large. With discounted values, the single CSAS is predicted to decrease AFDC families by 9.1% (slightly higher than 8.4% with market values); and to increase the mean hours by 7% among those on AFDC (compared to the counterpart of 6.1%) (see Table 5-7, panel 1). The children's allowance of $1000 with discounted medical values is estimated to have larger impacts on AFDC (16% compared to 13% decline) and on the mean hours (7.1% compared to 3.8% increase) (see panel 2). This is primarily because the discount rate gives Medicaid recipients less value of Medicaid than its market value. Perceiving Medicaid at the lesser values, those on AFDC are more likely to move off the program and go to work.

For the simulation involving NHI, both current medical coverage and NHI are discounted together. From the single program of NHI, the estimated anti-poverty effects are sensitive to how health coverage is valuated. With market values, NHI alone is estimated to reduce the poverty gap by 32.3%. With discounted values, however, this percent reduction goes down to 19.2%. This sensitivity is also found in the anti-poverty effect of the three-combined regime, but in much less degree. The three-combined reform (Table 5-7, final panel) indicates a 61.4% reduction (with market values) and about 50% reduction (with discounted values) in the poverty gap. Also, the discounted values result in a lesser effect on income redistribution, but not much different. Other effects, however, are not sensitive to values of coverage.

In conclusion, the sensitivity test reveals that the combined regime still reduces the degree of poverty by half, even from the most conservative point regarding valuation of medical benefits. However, estimated other effects are quite insensitive to the valuation of health care benefits.

Table 5-7
Results With Discounted Health Care Values

	[a] Estimated With Market Values	[b] Estimated With Discounted Values
CSAS of $2000 (Under Medium Improvement)		
% Chg in Pov Gap	-9.0	-8.9
% Chg in AFDC Cases	-8.4	-9.1
% Chg in FS Cases	-2.0	-2.0
% Chg in Mean Hrs [c]	6.1; -0.6; -0.5	7.0; -0.6; -0.5
Gini Coeff.	0.336	0.342
Children's Allowance of $1000		
% Chg in Pov Gap	-21.6	-20.4
% Chg in AFDC Cases	-13.0	-16.0
% Chg in FS Cases	-4.2	-4.8
% Chg in Mean Hrs [c]	3.8; -1.6; -1.6	7.1; -1.6; -1.5
Gini Coeff.	0.333	0.336
National Health Insurance		
% Chg in Pov Gap	-32.3	-19.2
% Chg in AFDC Cases	-2.0	-3.0
% Chg in FS Cases	-1.3	-1.5
% Chg in Mean Hrs [c]	-1.8; -1.3; -1.3	-0.1; -0.7; -0.7
Gini Coeff.	0.322	0.331
Three Combined: CSAS ($2000 & Medium), CA ($1000) & NHI		
% Chg in Pov Gap	-61.4	-49.8
% Chg in AFDC Cases	-33.9	-33.9
% Chg in FS Cases	-8.6	-8.4
% Chg in Mean Hrs [c]	18.3; -3.2; -2.9	18.5; -2.5; -2.2
Gini Coeff.	0.304	0.314

Table 5-7 Continues

Notes:
- [a] Values of medical coverage are equal to its cost of provision.
- [b] Market values of coverage are discounted by 0.58.
- [c] Percent change for AFDC, non-AFDC, and all parents, respectively.

Sensitivity to Labor Supply Model

Another sensitivity issue can be raised for a labor supply model and the parameters employed in that model. Wong (1988) and Meyer et al. (1991a), who used the same labor supply model, tested the sensitivity to alternative parameters. Rather than conducting another sensitivity test, I present the results from a simulation model which does not allow labor supply changes in response to policy changes. To see how the estimates are sensitive to labor supply responses (and also to see the magnitude of bias due to a possible model specification error),[9] Table 5-8 compares selected results from the labor supply simulation with those from the no labor supply simulation. As shown in the table, the estimated effects on the poverty gap, and AFDC and food stamp participation are very close in all sets of simulation (less than 1% difference). The gross cost for CSAS is estimated slightly higher with the labor supply model than the no labor supply model. The reason for the higher cost is that if we allow labor supply changes, AFDC mothers are more likely to work off welfare and participate in CSAS. On the other hand, net cost estimates vary somewhat from the labor supply to the no labor supply simulation. Although the predicted effects are insensitive, net cost estimates appear more sensitive to labor supply simulation, because a net cost incorporates all components of costs and savings in dollar figures. There are many sources of causing differences in net costs. First, the net cost incorporates the savings from welfare programs (AFDC, food stamps, and Medicaid): lesser dollar amounts of savings result when labor supply responses are constrained not to change. Second, a tax revenue gain or loss (from income and payroll taxes), and a EITC cost are closely associated with a change in earnings as a result of labor supply simulation. In general, fewer taxes are collected under the labor supply simulation, because individuals decrease their labor supply as a whole. In brief, higher estimates for a net cost from the labor supply simulation than those from the no labor

Table 5-8
Results From No Labor Supply Simulation

	Estimated From Labor Supply Simulation	Estimated From No Labor Supply Simulation
CSAS of $2000 (Under Medium Improvement)		
% Chg in Pov Gap	-9.0	-8.8
% Chg in AFDC Cases	-8.4	-7.7
% Chg in FS Cases	-2.0	-1.8
Gross Cost ($ million)	$ 2,153	$ 2,124
Net Cost ($ million)	$ -358	$ -1,288
Children's Allowance of $1000		
% Chg in Pov Gap	-21.6	-22.0
% Chg in AFDC Cases	-13.0	-12.6
% Chg in FS Cases	-4.2	-4.0
Gross Cost ($ million)	$ 67,988	$ 67,988
Net Cost ($ million)	$ 0	$ -4,769
National Health Insurance		
% Chg in Pov Gap	-32.3	-32.7
% Chg in AFDC Cases	-2.0	-0.6
% Chg in FS Cases	-1.3	-0.2
Gross Cost ($ million)	$ 104,121	$ 104,121
Net Cost ($ million)	$ 0	$ -1,855
Three Combined: CSAS ($2000 & Medium), CA ($1000) & NHI		
% Chg in Pov Gap	-61.4	-60.6
% Chg in AFDC Cases	-33.9	-31.2
% Chg in FS Cases	-8.6	-8.5
Gross Cost ($ million)	$ 175,305	$ 175,228
Net Cost ($ million)	$ 1,002	$ -6,718

supply simulation indicate that greater welfare savings do not outweigh lower tax revenues. Therefore, we can interpret the net costs estimated from the labor supply model as the conservative estimates.

Comparing Estimates with Other Studies

Table 5-9 displays a comparison of estimates for some selected outcomes with those estimated by other, prior studies. The estimates for CSAS are most comparable with Meyer, Garfinkel, Robins, and Oellerich (1991a). In particular, CSAS of $2000 assured level under the medium improvement assumption is selected for a comparison purpose. Also, my results (presented in Table 5-9) are obtained from the restricted sample of custodial families, because Meyer et al. (1991a) includes only these families. For children's allowance, the allowance of $1000 simulated by Meyer, Phillips, and Maritato (1991b) is selected to compare with the estimates of this study. From these comparisons, a large difference is found, particularly in the estimated effects on AFDC participation and labor supply, and in the gross cost estimates.

With respect to the effects on AFDC participation, Meyer et al. (1991a) predicted a 20% decline in AFDC caseloads due to the $2000 assured benefit of CSAS and medium improvement in child support (see Table 5-9, row 2). Their estimate is more than twice larger than my estimate of 9.8% at the same run of CSAS. Also, my estimated effects of the children's allowance on AFDC participation are much lower than those estimated by Meyer et al. (1991b). My study predicts that the children's allowance of $1000 would decrease AFDC families by 13%. On the other hand, a 23.6% decrease is predicted by Meyer et al.(1991b), which is almost twice as large. As discussed in chapter 3, these larger estimates in both prior studies of CSAS and children's allowance by Meyer et al. (1991a, 1991b) presumably result from ignoring Medicaid values linked to AFDC recipiency in their simulation models. This possibility is supported by my sensitivity test to discounted values of health care coverage. We have seen in Table 5-7 that an estimated reduction in AFDC caseloads is larger with discounted values than with market values. Put another way, if the current categorical nature of Medicaid recipiency is replaced with a universal health coverage available to all individuals, the predicted impact of CSAS or children's allowance on AFDC participation would be as high as the estimates of Meyer et. al.(1991a, 1991b). Given the current benefit package of AFDC with Medicaid, however, the estimated effects on AFDC in this study provide a downward correction of their overstated impact.

Table 5-9
Comparison Of Estimates With Other Studies

	CSAS: $2000 & Medium		Children's Allowance: $1000	
	My Estimate[a]	Meyer et al.[b]	My Estimate	Meyer et al.[c]
% Chg in Pov Gap	-18.6	-17.0	-21.6	-23.9
% Chg in AFDC Cases	-9.8	-20.0	-13.0	-23.6
% Chg in FS Cases	-2.7	n.a	-4.2	-3.7
% Chg in Mean Hrs - AFDC - nonAFDC - All	10.2 -2.7 -2.3	28.0 -3.0 0.0	3.8 -1.6 -1.6	13.9 n.a n.a
Total Cost ($mill) [d]	$ 2,153	$ 1,312	$ 67,988	$ 72,746

Notes:
[a] Estimated from the restricted sample of custodial families.
[b] Estimated by Meyer, Garfinkel, Robins & Oellerich (1991a).
[c] Estimated by Meyer, Phillips, & Maritato (1991b).
[d] For comparisons, all dollars amounts are expressed in 1988 terms.

When the effects on labor supply are compared with other studies, the positive effects particularly for the AFDC group are estimated in much smaller magnitudes. This study predicts that CSAS ($2000 and medium scenario) would increase the mean hours by 10.2% among those on AFDC (see Table 5-9, row 4). This estimate is almost three times lower than its counterpart--a 28% increase predicted by the Meyer et al. study (1991b) on CSAS. Similarly, the estimated impact of the children's allowance on the labor supply responses of AFDC parents is also much lower than that predicted by Meyer et al. (1991b)--a 3.8% increase compared to a 13.9% increase (almost 4 times as large). As for AFDC participation, the same explanation can be made for these differences in the labor supply effect for the AFDC group. In other words, when a Medicaid value is taken into account in the simulation model, an AFDC case is likely to lose more benefits if it exits the program. Thus, AFDC cases are more likely to choose welfare over work. Ignoring Medicaid values in the decision of welfare or work might result in a large increase in hours worked among AFDC parents, as shown in those prior studies.

On the other hand, my estimates for the anti-poverty effect are relatively similar to those in other studies. For the anti-poverty effect of CSAS, this study estimates a 18.6% reduction in the poverty gap, while Meyer et al.(1991a) indicates a slightly lower estimate (17% reduction) (see Table 5-9, row 1). Meyer et al. (1991a) also estimated a decrease in the poverty rate by 6% and a reduction in the gap by 9% under the $3000 level of benefit with the current child support assumption (not presented in the table). This study again predicts similar effects: a 7.7% reduction in the poverty incidence and an 8.4 reduction in the poverty gap under the same level of assurance with current child support (not presented in the table). Generally, my estimates for the anti-poverty effects are close to those in the Meyer et al. study (1991a) at all other levels of assured benefit and at different assumptions of child support. On the other hand, my estimates under the $3000 CSAS (current) are larger than those estimated by Lerman (1989). Lerman (1989) predicted that the Wisconsin CSAS[10] at $3000 under current child support would decrease the poverty rate by 3% and the gap by 4%, indicating much lower effects than my estimates. However, another comparison reveals almost identical anti-poverty effects. Lerman (1989) estimated a 1% decrease in the poverty rate and a 2% reduction in the poverty gap under the assurance of $1080 assuming current child support. In this study, the assured benefit of

$1000 under no improvement in child support is estimated to decrease the poverty rate by 1% and the poverty gap by 2.3% (not presented in the table), indicating almost the same estimates. Also, the estimated anti-poverty effects of children's allowance in this study are close to those predicted by Meyer et al.(1991b). Meyer at al.(1991b) estimated that the allowance of $1000 would reduce the poverty rate by 14.6% and the gap by 23.9%. The same plan in this study results in a 15.3% decline in the poverty rate and a 21.6% reduction in the poverty gap.

The final row of Table 5-9 shows a comparison of estimated gross costs. Compared to the Meyer et al.(1991a) study on CSAS, the gross costs for CSAS are estimated higher in this study. This study estimates $2.2 billion for the $2000 assured benefit under the medium scenario, while Meyer et al.(1991a) estimated $1.3 billion (converted to the 1988 dollar amount). The same pattern is found under the no improvement scenario. CSAS under no improvement is estimated to have gross costs in the range of $1 billion to $7.4 billion, depending on levels of assured benefit. This range of costs is compared with cost estimates of $0.7 billion to $6.5 billion from the Meyer et al. study (not presented in the table). Overall, my gross cost estimates are $1-2 billion higher than those estimated by Meyer et al. (1991a). The larger cost estimates of my study are a primary result of more custodial parents in the SIPP than in the CPS. The 1986 CPS, which was used in the Meyer et al. (1991a) study, indicates about 8.9 million custodial parents. On the other hand, the SIPP employed in this study counts 12.1 million as of 1988. Thus, the total number of custodial parents in the SIPP outnumbers that of CPS by 3.2 million. This explains the higher cost estimates for CSAS in this study. However, the gross cost of children's allowance ($1000) is estimated at $68 billion, which is lower than the $72.7 billion in the Meyer et al. (1991b) study on children's allowance. Different sample definitions seem to contribute to this gap. The sample of my study includes families with children only under the age of 18. On the other hand, the Meyer et al. study on children's allowance included those with children aged 19 to 24 if they had low earnings or were in school as well.

Notes

1.In 1988, the official poverty threshold for a family of two was $7,958; $9,435 for three; $12,092 for four, $14,305 for five; $16,149 for six; and $18,248 for seven or more persons.

2.The mean hours decrease very slightly as the level of assured benefit increases. However, they appear constant because of rounding.

3.Chapter 4 explained how I arrived at this figure.

4.Zedlewski et al. (1993), for example, assumed 23 % 'insurance effect' for individuals receiving first dollar coverage.

5.See Table 2 in Zedlewski et al. (1993).

6.The cost of Medicare is not counted. The small number of individuals covered through Medicare in the sample are assumed to continue Medicare coverage.

7.Given multiple payers under Clinton's proposal, significant administrative savings would not result from Clinton's plan. In addition, health care utilizations would not significantly increase if the use of "managed competition" for cost containment is successful under Clinton's proposal.

8.In 1988, total social welfare expenditures under the public programs were $885.8 billion and total government outlays were $1593.2 billion (U.S. Bureau of the Census, 1991, Table No. 581). The estimated total cost of $155.4 billion for the combined programs (after subtracting associated welfare and EITC savings), under the medium assumption, would imply increases in social welfare expenditures by 17.5% and government outlays by 9.7%.

9.The utility formulation for two-parent families adopted from Meyer et al. (1991b) appears to have a specification error. A couple of sample cases suggest this possibility, but tracking down the error is beyond my time constraint because it was found after all results were obtained. This is another reason that I present the results from the no labor supply model in order to see the magnitude of bias due to that possibility.

10. A wage subsidy and a surtax on custodial parent's income are included for Wisconsin CSAS simulation.

VI

Conclusion

Major Findings

This study has analyzed the economic effects of the combined non-income-tested transfers for families with children. As an alternative approach to assisting poor children, three policy changes have been proposed, all providing non-income-tested benefits: (a) replacing the current child support system with a child support assurance system (CSAS); (b) replacing income tax deductions for children with a children's allowance; (c) replacing Medicaid and employer-provided insurance with a national health insurance (NHI). By introducing these combined non-income-tested programs, I assume that there will be a shift in the transfer regime for families with children from 'income-tested' to 'non-income-tested.' One goal of this study has been to estimate what benefits would result at what cost when the new regime is implemented. Based on the labor supply simulation model, answers to the following research questions have been estimated:

(1) What would be the poverty incidence and gap under the three combined programs of the non-income-tested regime, compared to those under the current income-tested regime?

(2) How much would non-income-tested programs decrease AFDC caseloads and save AFDC benefits? As a result, how much would off-AFDC cases subsequently decrease Medicaid recipiency and its expenditures?

(3) What impact would the non-income-tested regime have on food stamp participation and its benefit expenditures?

(4) What effects would the three non-income-tested programs have on income redistribution?

(5) What impact would they have on the labor supply?

(6) What would be the total cost? When financing schedules and savings are taken into account, what would be the net cost to the public?

(7) Is there any interaction effect when non-income-tested programs are combined?

The results are summarized as follows. If the three non-income-tested programs (CSAS at the $2000 assured benefit, children's allowance at the $1000, and NHI) are implemented together, poverty among families with children would be substantially reduced. The poverty rate is estimated to decline by the range of 43% to 51%; the poverty gap would decrease by the range of 54% to 61%, depending on assumptions of private child support. It should be noted that these anti-poverty effects can be achieved, even if payroll taxes for NHI financing are not exempted for the poor. The combined regime is also predicted to significantly decrease welfare participation. The three non-income-tested programs would decrease AFDC caseloads by the range of 21% to 34%, and decrease the number of families receiving food stamps by the range of 6% to 9%, depending on child support assumptions. Consequently, AFDC benefit expenditures would decrease by 40-50%; food stamps expenditures would decrease by the range of 18% to 25% (depending on assumptions). Current skewness of income distribution is also smoothed under the combined non-income-tested programs. Using the medium assumption, the share of the bottom two quintiles would increase from 17.8% to 20.4% (a 2.6 point increase), whereas the top quintile would decrease its income share from 39.8% to 37.5% (a 2.3 point decrease). This equalizing effect on income distribution is summarized as a decrease in the Gini coefficient: from 0.343 to 0.304 (a more than 11% decrease). The predicted efficiency loss due to the combined non-income-tested programs is not very large. The average hours worked by all parents would decrease by the range of 2.6% to 2.9%, depending on assumptions used. On the other hand, the combined programs are predicted to have large incentives for parents on AFDC to work: mean hours worked by all AFDC parents would increase by the range of 11% to 18%; and, in particular, 6-10% of nonworking parents on AFDC would begin to work under the combined regime.

Interaction effects are found in some outcome measures, when the three non-income-tested programs are combined. Among parents on AFDC, the labor supply results indicate that the combined programs would produce a strong upward interaction for the positive effects on their hours worked: the combined regime yields a 27 hour increase in the mean hours over the addition of single programs' mean hours--more than twice as many hours. Particularly, the three combined programs provide spring-board incentives for non-working AFDC parents to go to work. Under the combined programs, 10.3% of non-working AFDC parents are predicted to start work; this work incentive effect is 5 times as large as the sum of single effects (2.3%). Among all parents, as expected, the overall effects on their labor supply are negative (a decrease in the mean hours) under the combined programs. This study, however, has predicted that the combined programs would create a downward interaction for the negative effects on the labor supply: the overall negative effects on all parents' labor supply responses are weakened by 20% under the combined regime. This finding implies that a combined universal income guarantee would not result in a proportionate efficiency loss as the level of guarantee increases.

Interaction effects are also found in AFDC participation and poverty measures. When the three programs are combined, the impact on AFDC reduction becomes substantially strengthened due to the interaction of programs: the combined regime yields a 10 percentage points greater reduction over the addition of single programs' effects (using the medium assumption). Similarly, the three-combined programs become more effective as an anti-poverty means: achieving a 5 percentage points greater reduction in the poverty rate.

Gross cost estimates for three non-income-tested programs are as follows: CSAS at the $2000 assured benefit would require a gross cost of $3-4 billion (depending on child support assumptions); the children's allowance would cost $68 billion; and NHI would require a cost of $104 billion. The total gross cost for these three programs would be in the range of $175 billion to $176 billion. This cost can be financed through welfare savings (between $18-20 billion), income tax revenue ($74-75 billion from eliminating personal exemptions for children, increasing the income tax rate by 2.7%, taxing public benefits themselves, and repealing tax exemptions for employer premium contribution), and payroll tax revenue ($81 billion from creating a new payroll tax of 7.1%). With these tax revenues and welfare savings taken into account, the net cost arrived at is $1-2.6 billion, depending on child support assumptions. This net cost is required for implementing the CSAS of $2000 assured benefit.

As mentioned in chapter 4 (methods section), the market-value approach, which has been employed to valuate health insurance coverage, in general overstates the gain in the recipient's economic well-being. Thus, a sensitivity test to values of health care coverage is conducted from the most conservative point of view regarding valuation of medical benefits. In particular, the predicted impacts on poverty and Gini coefficient appear slightly sensitive to discounted values, although the differences are not large. With discounted values, the combined regime is predicted to reduce the poverty gap by 50% (compared to 61.4% with market values), and decrease the Gini coefficient from .343 to .314 (compared to .304 with market values). However, estimated other effects of the combined regime are quite insensitive to discounted values of coverage. With discounted values, the predicted effects on AFDC and food stamp caseloads, and on labor supply are almost identical with those with market values. Also, the results from the no labor supply simulation indicate that the labor supply model does not change the estimates significantly.

Contributions

This is the first effort in research on the costs and benefits of three non-income-tested programs. Although some researchers have assessed the effects of a single program, no empirical research has been conducted to estimate the costs and effects of those programs combined. As an alternative approach to improve children's economic well-being in the U.S., the research results provide valuable information for policy makers for redirecting income transfer policy for families with children.

Second, one of research questions has focused on whether three non-income-tested programs would produce any interaction effect, when they are combined. As mentioned above, I have found that the combined regime produce the upward effects on reducing welfare caseloads and poverty. Particularly, the combined non-income-tested programs create spring-board incentives for parents on AFDC to increase their work efforts due to the interaction of programs. As expected, for all parents, an overall negative effect on their labor supply exists, but this study has found a downward interaction for the negative effects on the labor supply. This implies that a combined universal income guarantee would not result in a proportionate efficiency loss as the level of guarantee increases. These findings are new and different from other prior studies.

Third, this study has amended a methodological drawback which has been found in prior simulation studies. Previous research on CSAS (and children's allowance) ignored the benefit package of Medicaid and food stamps which is closely linked to AFDC recipiency. Ignoring Medicaid and food stamps is expected to overestimate the program's effects on AFDC participation and labor supply. Indeed, this study has found that the effect of CSAS on AFDC participation estimated by Meyer et al. (1991a) is overstated twice as large (compared to my estimate under medium assumption); and that the effect of children's allowance on AFDC caseloads estimated by Meyer et al. (1991b) is overstated almost twice as large (compared to my estimate). Similarly, compared to my predicted effects on labor supply among parents on AFDC, an increase in the mean hours has been even more overestimated by prior studies on CSAS and children's allowance--3-4 times as large. This study, thus, provides a downward correction of the overestimated impact on AFDC participation and labor supply of previous studies.

Fourth, this study has corrected the undercounted number of custodial parents in the data, and thus provided a more precise cost estimate for CSAS. Most prior studies on CSAS, because of data limitations, missed the following groups of custodial parents: (a) mothers who had no children from the most recent divorce or separation but had children from an earlier divorce or separation; (b) mothers who are currently married but had children out of wedlock; and (c) custodial fathers. These undercounts primarily may have resulted in underestimating the gross cost of CSAS in other studies. In this study, however, those missing custodial parents are included through using the topical modules on household relationships as well as child support in the SIPP data. As expected, my estimate for the total number of custodial parents (12.1 million including both mothers and fathers) is much larger than that of the CPS data (9.4 million including only mothers).[1] When compared only for the total number of custodial mothers, this study has found that CPS undercounts the number of custodial mothers by 1.3 million, although CPS additionally includes those living with children aged between 18 and 21. As a result, the gross cost for CSAS is estimated at $1-2 billion higher than that of Meyer et al. (1991a).

Finally, this study has estimated the effects of national health insurance on poverty and income distribution in terms of its benefit structure. Although health reforms have been a big issue across the country, no study has been conducted to analyze NHI's effects through its benefit structure on poverty and income distribution. Also, no study has simulated labor supply changes in response to universal health care benefits and increased tax rates under NHI. The results from the single program of NHI indicate that NHI would be a more effective tool than any other single program for reducing poverty and income inequality. Although the poor are required to pay the same rate of payroll taxes for financing NHI, one-third of the current poverty gap can be reduced by NHI alone when health care benefits are considered. Similarly, even if payroll taxes imply a regressive financing schedule, this study has found that NHI would still reduce the income inequality coefficient from .343 to .322. This redistributional effect is larger than any other plan of CSAS or children's allowance.

Limitations

Despite its improvements on previous research, this study is limited in several areas. Its estimates should be interpreted in light of the following shortcomings.

The first limitation concerns the labor supply simulation model employed for the analysis. The simulation model leaves out two important elements for labor supply responses. First, the demand side of labor is ignored. In other words, the simulation allows labor supply changes as if parents who choose to start working or increase their work level could always do so. In the real world, they may be constrained by the availability of suitable jobs in the market. The parents who are more likely to be constrained by the demand side are those with low earnings capacity, especially AFDC mothers who wish to leave welfare through work (Wong, 1988, p.231). Therefore, ignoring labor demand could possibly draw a more optimistic conclusion on the success of the reform for low-income individuals.

Second, the simulation also assumes that parents who wish to decrease hours of work could always do so. In reality, their work decisions may be constrained by a job requirement for certain hours, and may be more affected by community values or a sense of self-achievement through work rather than a simple utility count (particularly among middle and upper class persons). This aspect of labor supply decision is not captured by the simulation model. It should be noted, however, that these two elements ignored in the simulation model have opposite forces that counteract bias. In other words, a somewhat optimistic conclusion as a result of ignoring labor demand (first element) could be mitigated by ignoring the work hours constraint (the second element).

In addition to the demand side of the labor market, this study has ignored macro effects of policy changes. Microsimulation, which has been employed in this study, is based on a static model which primarily analyzes the first-round impact of policy changes on income, taxes, and individual behaviors at the household level. However, any policy change could have "wave" effects on the second-, third- and fourth-round, beyond the scope of individual households, for example, on the price system and other economic systems such as industries, regions, and occupations. Estimating these macro effects is beyond the scope of this study.

Another limitation of this study is related to the behavior response of absent parents. As addressed in chapter 4 (methods section), CSAS reform requires higher taxes on absent parents' incomes in the form of child support. The use of the percentage standard and immediate income withholding virtually means a new or higher tax rate for absent parents. Thus, the reform presumably will affect absent parents' labor supply decisions. However, this study has ignored this possible effect of CSAS on their work behaviors.

Increasing private child support has two conceptual effects on the absent parent's work decision (Wong, 1988, p.232). An increase in private child support leads to a lower reward for an hour's work and thus the less expensive price of leisure. Due to this substitution effect, absent parents may choose leisure over work. At the same time, with a loss of income through increased child support, the net income of the absent parent decreases. This income effect leads absent parents to increase work to compensate for the loss of income. Since these two components have opposite effects on the labor supply of absent parents, the net labor supply effect is an empirical question. If it turns out that the net effect is negative (work less), my estimates of child support collection would be overstated, and thus CSAS costs would be underestimated. The opposite would be true if the net effect is positive (work more). In any case, the existing economic literature indicates that absent parents, who are likely to be the male heads of their new households, are less responsive to a change in tax rate than custodial mothers (Wong, 1988, p. 233).

In addition, this study ignores changes in absent parents' incomes for the effects on poverty and income redistribution. Thus, the percent reduction in poverty may be overestimated because of ignoring income losses of noncustodial parents, and redistributional effects may be underestimated because of ignoring income redistribution from noncustodial to custodial families.

This study is also limited with respect to the valuation method of health care coverage. As described in chapter 4 (methods section), the market-value approach--a method developed mainly for valuating public coverage--has been employed to valuate health insurance coverage. In general, this approach overstates the gain in the recipient's economic well-being (Smeeding, 1982, p.27), because of limited market exchange. Private insurance coverage provided through employers is also problematic, "because different tax treatments, risk pooling, and coverage options are involved" (Wolfe & Moffitt, 1991, p. 387). To capture the recipient's own true value, Wolfe and Moffitt (1991) suggest that a cash-equivalent valuation method is preferable (p.388). This method calculates "a cash-equivalent value of health care by assuming a particular utility function and then imputing to broad groups of individuals (by income, for example) an average amount that they would be willing to pay for the care" (Wolfe and Moffitt, 1991, p.388). However, the use of this method is a difficult task, requiring estimation of the parameters of the utility function (Wolfe and Moffitt, 1991, p.388).

As a compromise, this study has conducted a sensitivity test by discounting market-values by 0.58. However, some economists have argued that the recipient's relative values are different under different public programs (e.g., Medicaid and Medicare) (see Smeeding, 1982). It is expected that the recipient values are even more different between public coverage and private coverage. Since we lack empirical evidence of how much the values differ from public to private coverage, I have applied to all types of health care coverage the same discount rate of 0.58, which is the lowest estimate of recipient value of cash equivalence from the existing literature. This simplification may have lead to some bias in my sensitivity-test results.

There is also another limitation in my valuation method. The use of mean values misses many important interfamily differences that affect valuations for health insurance. According to Wolfe and Moffitt (1991), recipients have different values depending on "health status, the number of persons covered, expected utilization of medical care, the cost of medical care in the community, and intensity of coverage" (p.388). In this study, mean market-values of coverage have been adjusted only for age groups (the aged and nonaged) and the number of persons covered in the family, leaving out other factors affecting a recipient's different valuation.

With respect to NHI cost estimates, two limitations should be mentioned. First, no increase in health care utilization is considered under NHI. Because NHI has been proposed to provide the same benefit package as the average level of current employer-provided insurance, and to require the same rate of coinsurance, currently insured individuals are not expected to significantly increase their utilization levels. However, currently uninsured individuals would increase utilization in response to first-dollar coverage. Second, administrative savings associated with a single payer system are not considered. Since the administrative savings seem larger than the cost increase due to utilization changes, my cost estimate of $104 billion for NHI to provide universal coverage for all families with children might be overstated. As discussed in chapter 5, the seemingly over-estimated total cost is adopted without a downward adjustment, leaving an overestimated residual for transition costs for many uncertain changes from NHI implementation. Therefore, my cost estimate for NHI should be taken as near the upper bound, providing conservative estimation.

With respect to NHI, this study also may overestimate increases in wages at the bottom of income distribution as a result of NHI implementation. Under NHI, current employer-paid premiums have been converted into increased wages, under the assumption that employers would shift their premium savings directly to workers. However, employers of low-wage workers may be unwilling to shift back their savings to workers. In addition, this study has ignored current health-care transfers through uncompensated care. In general, uncompensated care under the current system implies medical transfers from the insured to the uninsured, because providers usually shift these costs to patients with coverage. Ignoring this type of current health care transfer may result in overestimated effects of NHI on poverty and income redistribution.

The simulation results have been obtained through many intermediate steps including statistical estimation. Because of data limitations, for example, statistical equations have been estimated for nonworker's hourly wage rate, the probability of award, collection rate, and child support payment. Also, absent parents' incomes have been imputed according to equation estimates by Garfinkel and Oellerich (1989); labor supply parameters have been adopted particularly from estimates by Johnson and Pencaval (1984). Since the simulation has been built upon these estimated equations, the results may be sensitive to the specification of equation models and the estimated parameters.

The final limitation of this study is related to its scope rather than its methodology. The focus of this study has been on an economic assessment of non-income-tested programs. A variety of issues are involved with the issue of income-testing and non-income-testing, including their effects on family structure, stigma, social cohesion, and fostering bureaucracy. This research cannot provide a comprehensive assessment covering all these questions. The evaluation of non-income-tested reform, thus, is limited in the sense that my assessment is made on its economic performance and ignoring its other non-economic effects. In addition, administrative cost factors are not considered for assessing the economic effects of non-income-tested programs.

Some cautions are needed if policy implications for the year of 1993 are to be drawn from my results estimated based on the year of 1988. During these five years, the world has been changing and some new policies have become effective. In particular, the following changes should be remembered in order to apply my estimates for the current year. First, health care costs have been dramatically increasing. This change would imply an underestimation of employers' premium contribution and NHI costs for the year of 1993. Second, beginning in early 1990, Medicaid coverage became mandatory for children under the age of 6 and pregnant women with incomes below 133% of the poverty line. In particular, enrollment rates for children should increase in the long run, as the 1990 legislation takes effect by 2002,[2] As Medicaid coverage gradually expands to poor children based on the income standard, the categorical nature of the Medicaid program, by which eligibility was tied to AFDC, will eventually disappear (by

2002). This change implies that Medicaid benefits eventually will not have the incentive effect for AFDC recipients to stay in the program. Since this study has considered Medicaid's disincentives in the prediction of AFDC participation and work decisions, my estimated effects on AFDC participation and labor supply may be understated for drawing implications for the 1990s. Third, the earned income tax credit (EITC) has changed since 1988. The Omnibus Budget Reconciliation Act of 1990 (OBRA 1990) substantially increased the maximum amount of the basic credit and added an adjustment to reflect family size (Green Book, 1991, p. 897). Therefore, estimated EITC amounts in this study might be under what would be in 1993.

Conclusion

The U.S. public transfer system for families with children has two pronounced characteristics: (a) most public programs are strongly income-tested in that, to be eligible, a family must have income below a certain standard level, and benefits significantly decline as earnings or other income sources increase; and (b) they are categorical in the sense that benefits are more restricted to a certain type of family (i.e., female-headed) and entitlement is closely linked among several welfare programs. During the last two decades, we have witnessed that this welfare/categorical nature of the transfer approach is a major source of controversy and criticism. Numerous research projects have been devoted to proving, in particular, to what degree welfare programs discourage work efforts and contribute to marital break-ups and out-of-wedlock births. Moffitt's review (1990) of the literature suggests that the AFDC program reduces work by 30% (based on a midpoint estimate); and that the estimated effects on female headship are generally very small in magnitude. However, the exact magnitude does not seem to be the point of criticism. Whether the actual effects of welfare programs are large or small depends on interpretation (Ellwood, 1988). More importantly, as suggested by Ellwood (1988), welfare programs contain fundamental conflicts with basic value tenets of American society--the autonomy of the individual, the virtue of work, the primacy of the family, the sense of community (pp. 18-26).

Ellwood (1988) points out that "welfare could discourage work for two conceptually different reasons: it reduces the pressure to work;

and it reduces the rewards of working" (p.19). Conservatives often argue that welfare gives mothers the opportunity to stay home and raise their children rather than be forced to work to keep their family at a subsistence level (Mead, 1986). Certainly the alternative support of welfare for work decreases the urgency that an individual needs to take any kind of job. In addition, the amount of benefits will decrease as a poor mother begins to work and increase earnings. According to calculations by Ellwood (1988), based on a typical AFDC case in the medium state, an AFDC mother would effectively keep only $1.35 per hour from her $6-per-hour job after taking into account child care costs, income taxes, and earned income tax credits (p. 138). Furthermore, if she works, she would lose her Medicaid benefits. This demonstrates that a welfare mother is essentially worse off financially if she is working. This is why conservatives argue that the U.S. welfare system fosters dependency rather than self-sufficiency through work.

Ellwood (1988) also points out that the U.S. welfare system goes against the value of family. It provides much more public support to poor, single-parent families than to poor, two-parent families. The current system virtually leaves children living in poor, working, two-parent families without protection. We know that the rate of poverty is relatively lower for children living in two-parent families than for those in single-parent families. However, half the poor children live in two-parent families (U.S. Bureau of the Census, 1992, p.110), because many more children live in two-parent families than in single-parent ones. Why are these two-parent families living in poverty? Ellwood claims that work alone can not explain poverty among two-parent families. The vast majority of two-parent families are full-time working families: only 6% fall into the partially employed or unemployed; and only 1% of families have two healthy parents who both report no work at all during the year (Ellwood, 1988, p.88). Surprisingly, full-time working families make up 44% of the poor, two-parent families (Ellwood, 1988, p.88). This indicates that work does not always ensure that a family will escape poverty. It also indicates that low wages are a major culprit of poverty among these families. For example, for a family of three a full-time minimum wage job does not provide even a poverty-line living (Ellwood, 1988, p.89). In addition, as discussed in chapter 1, the lack of access to health care among children is the most serious for those living with working, poor parents. These families follow the family value and the work ethic that traditional society has long cherished (Ellwood, 1988), but they remain in poverty with no health care protection. As often criticized, the U.S. welfare system clearly does not reinforce this type of family.

The problem with such a system is that most people believe that the more generous benefits to single mothers may encourage families to break up and induce women to have children out of wedlock. Logically, there is no question that the welfare system reduces "the cost of being in single-parent families" (Ellwood, 1988, p.22). And although much research has found that welfare programs have had little effect on the family structure (Moffitt, 1990), most people tend to believe their own subjective thinking rather than the objective research findings (Ellwood, 1988).

Also, the welfare approach undermines the value of community (Ellwood, 1988). A conventional approach of transfer policy is to direct resources to those in the greatest need. However, as mentioned by Ellwood, "targeting can label and stigmatize recipients, and the poor are marked as different," because only they receive the "special treatment" of public support, and that difference is accompanied by a negative implication. Ellwood further addresses that in our welfare system the implication seems to be that people on welfare are "deficient in some way," and that the failure of those on welfare often seems to be perceived by both sides--the recipients as well as the 'givers' at large. Ellwood argues that "the more public assistance targets the poor, the more they are isolated and segregated from the rest of society (p.23-25)." I believe that our longstanding welfare dilemma is a inevitable consequence of over-targeting welfare policy.

I also agree with the point made by Ellwood (1988) that the recent conservative critique of the welfare system essentially comes from these inherent value conflicts of welfare with major American society, rather than its actual adverse effects. All marginal welfare reforms have failed to solve these inevitable conflicts between welfare and the American value system. That is why welfare reforms during the last two decades have ended up only in dissatisfaction and have created more tensions.

Is there any way to find a solution for welfare conflicts and, more importantly, a better provision for children's well-being? In searching for a way of helping out poor children and avoiding the helping dilemma that we face, I believe that the proposed three non-income-tested transfers can bring a solution. The proposed non-income-tested regime effectively provides more support to the working poor.

Since benefits are independent of earnings, they don't discourage work efforts. When parent's earnings are combined with the certain public guarantee, children will live in better economic circumstances. The results of this study indicate that the combined regime would reduce the degree of child poverty by almost two-thirds. In addition, the proposed regime establishes a more uniform transfer system that protects all children, regardless of their family status. The children's allowance and universal health care coverage imply that children deserve to receive public support as their right, regardless of their economic or family situation: children have a right not to be poor--a right to grow up with a reasonable level of protection. CSAS entails the strong message that parents must be responsible for supporting their own children whether or not they live together, and that the government has the responsibility for protecting children's minimum economic security. Clearly, such a system emphasizes a sense of shared responsibility for our children's well-being by both private and public parties. Neither does it stigmatize recipients, nor isolate them from the rest of society. It will nurture a sense of community.

Most importantly, children are our future human capital. We have found that child poverty has negative consequences for the next generation as well as for today's children: today's poor children are less likely to receive adequate nutrition and health care, less likely to complete high school, and less well-equipped as adults to support their own dependents, and the productivity of the workforce as a whole will suffer. The goal of public policies that reduce child poverty is to invest for the future, and produce a healthy, educated workforce prepared for the economic challenges of a competitive world in the next generation. Somewhat increased taxes to pay for this will be paid off in the higher productivity of the workforce in the future generation.

Notes

1. This estimate is based on April 1988. See the U.S. Bureau of Census (1990, June), Table B.

2. OBRA 1990 requires states to phase in coverage for children 6 to 19 years old in families with incomes up to 100% of the poverty line by 2002.

References

Anderson, R. & Newman, F. (1973). "Societal and Individual Determinants of Medical Care Utilization in the United States." *The Milbank Memorial Fund Quarterly*, 51(1): 95-124.

Arnett, R. H., Carol, C., Davidoff, L., & Freeland, M. (1985). "Health Spending Trends in the 1980's: Adjusting to Financial Incentives." *Health Care Financing Review*, 6(3): 1-26.

Bane, M. J. & Ellwood, D. (1986). "Slipping Into and Out of Poverty: the Dynamics of Spells." *Journal of Human Resources*, 21: 1-23.

Berkowitz, E. (1991). *America's Welfare State: From Roosevelt to Reagan*. Baltimore: The Johns Hopkins University Press.

Betson, D., Greenberg, D., & Kaston, R. (1982). A Simulation Analysis of the Economic Efficiency and Distributional Effects of Alternative Program Structures: the Negative Income Tax Versus the Credit Income Tax, In I. Garfinkel (ed.), *Income-tested Transfer Programs: The Case for and Against*. New York, NY: Academic Press.

Bianchi, S.M. (1990). "America's Children: Mixed Prospects." *Population Bulletin*, 45(1).

Bill Clinton for President Committee (1992). *Bill Clinton's American Health Care Plan: National Health Insurance Reform to Cut Costs and Cover Everybody*. Little Rock: Bill Clinton for President Committee.

Blank, R. (1989). "The Effect of Medical Need and Medicaid on AFDC Participation." *Journal of Human Resources*, 24: 54-87.

Blendon, R. B., Leitman, R., Morrison, I., & Donelan, K. (1990). "Satisfaction with Health Systems in Ten Countries." *Health Affair*, 9(2): 185-192.

Brazer, H. (1968). Tax Policy and Children's Allowance, In E. M. Burns (Ed.), *Children's Allowances and the Economic Welfare of Children* (The Report of a Conference, pp. 140-149). New York, NY: Citizen's Committee for Children of New York, Inc.

Briar, S. (1969). "Why Children's Allowances." *Social Work*, 14(1): 5-12.

Bronow, R. S., Beltran, R. A., Cohen, S. C., Elliott, P. T., Goldman, G. M., & Spotnitz, S. G. (1991). "The Physicians Who Care Plan." *Journal of the American Medical Association*, 265(19): 2511-2515.

Brook, R. H. et al. (1983). "Does Free Care Improve Adults' Health? Results from a Randomized Controlled Trial." *The New England Journal of Medicine*, 309(23): 1426-1434.

Brown, E. R. (1988). "Principles for a National Health Program: A Framework for Analysis and Development." *The Milbank Quarterly*, 66(4): 573-617.

Brown, L. D. (1992). "Policy Reform as Creative Destruction: Political and Administrative Challenges in Preserving the Public-Private Mix." *Inquiry*, 29(2): 188-202.

Buczko, W. (1989). "Hospital Utilization and Expenditures in a Medicaid Population." *Health Care Financing Review*, 11(1): 35-47.

Bumpass, L. (1985). "Children and Marital Disruption: A Replication and Update." *Demography*, 21: 71-82.

Burns, E. M. (1968). Childhood and the Children's Allowance. *Welfare Reform: Problems and Solutions*, Madison, WI: University of Wisconsin-Madison, Institute for Research on Poverty.

Burtless, G. (1986). The Work Response to a Guaranteed Income: A Survey of Experimental Evidence. In *Lessens from the Income Maintenance Experiment* (Conference Series No. 30). Boston: Federal Reserve Bank of Boston.

Butler, S. M. (1991, May). "A Tax Reform Strategy to Deal With the Uninsured." *Journal of the American Medical Association*, 265(19): 2541-2544.

Kansas Employer Coalition on Health (1991). "A Framework for Reform of the US Health Care Financing and Provision System." *Journal of the American Medical Association*, 265(19): 2529-2531.

Cain, G. & Watts, H. (eds.) (1973). *Income Maintenance and Labor Supply*, New York, NY: Academic Press.

Carroll, S. S. & Meyer, J. A. (1993). An Employment-Based System with Cost Controls: An Analysis of the Clinton and Mitchell Health Care Proposals, In J. A. Meyer & S. S. Carroll (Eds.), *Building Blocks for Change: How Health Care Affects Our Future* (pp. 209-249). Washington, DC: The Economic and Social Research Institute.

Cartland, J. & Yudkowsky, B. K. (1993). "State Estimates of Uninsured Children." *Health Affairs*, Spring: 144-151.

Center for National Health Program Studies (1992). *The National Health Program Chartbook*. Cambridge, MA: Harvard Medical School.

Congressional Budget Office (1990). *Reducing the Deficit: Spending and Revenue Options, Part II*. Washington, DC: U.S. Government Printing Office. 143-146.

Congressional Budget Office (1991). *Universal Health Insurance Coverage Using Medicare's Payment Rates*. Washington, DC: U.S. Government Printing Office.

Cooper, C & Katz, A. (1978). *The Cash Equivalent of In-Kind Income*. Stanford, Connecticut: Cooper and Company.

Corbett, T. (1993). "Child Poverty and Welfare Reform: Progress or Paralysis." *Focus*, 15(1): 1-17. Madison, WI: University of Wisconsin-Madison, Institute for Research on Poverty.

Cunningham, P. J. & Monheit, A. C. (1990). "Insuring the Children: A Decade of Change." *Health Affairs*, 9(4): 77-90.

Danziger, S. H. (1989a). *Antipoverty Policies and Child Poverty* (DP #884-89). Madison, WI: University of Wisconsin-Madison, Institute for Research on Poverty.

Danziger, S. H. (1989b). Fighting Poverty and Reducing Welfare Dependency, In P. H. Cottingham & D. T. Ellwood (Eds.), *Welfare Policy for the 1990s*. Cambridge, MA: Harvard University Press.

Danziger, S. H. & Gottschalk, P. (1986). How Are Families with Children Faring (DP #801-86). Madison, WI: University of Wisconsin-Madison, Institute for Research on Poverty.

Danziger, S. H. & Weinberg, D. H. (1992). *The Historical Record: Trends in Family Income, Inequality, and Poverty* (Conference Paper, May 28-30). Madison, WI: University of Wisconsin-Madison, Institute for Research on Poverty.

Danziger, S. H. & Weinberg, D. H. (1986) (eds.). *Fighting Poverty: What Works and What Doesn't*. Cambridge, MA: Harvard University Press.

Davidson, G. & Moscovice, I. (1989). "Health Insurance and Welfare Reentry." *Health Services Research*, 24(5): 599-614.

Davis, K. (1991). "Expanding Medicare and Employer Plans to Achieve Universal Health Insurance." *Journal of the American Medical Association*, 265(19): 2525-2528.

Davis, K. (1975). *National Health Insurance: Benefits, Costs and Consequences*. Washington, DC: The Brookings Institute.

Davis, K. & Schoen, C. (1978). *Health and the War on Poverty: A Ten-Year Appraisal*. Washington, DC: The Brookings Institute.

Davies, B. (1976). *Universality, Selectivity and Effectiveness in Social Policy*. London: Heineman and Company.

Dept. of Health Policy and Management (1991). "Caring for the Uninsured: Choices for Reform." *Journal of the American Medical Association*, 265(19): 2563-2565.

Dor, A., Hunt-McCool, J. C., & Johnson, A. (1992). The Effect of Health Insurance Coverage on the Labor Supply of Married Women. Preliminary Manuscript.

Duncan, G., Coe, R., & Hill, M. (1984). The Dynamic of Poverty, In G. Duncan (ed.), *Years of Poverty, Years of Plenty*, Ann Arbor, MI: University of Michigan, Survey Research Center.

Duncan, G. & Hoffman, S. D. (1985). "A Reconsideration of the Economic Consequences of Marital Dissolution." *Demography*, 22(November): 485-98.

Ellwood, D.T. (1988). *Poor Support: Poverty in the American Family*. New York, NY: Basic Books.

Enterline, P. E., Salter, V., McDonald, A. D., & McDonald, J. C. (1973). "The Distribution of Medical Services Before and After 'Free' Medical Care: the Quebec Experience." *New England Journal of Medicine*, 289: 1174-1178.

Enthoven, A. C. & Kronick, R. (1991). "Universal Health Insurance Through Incentives Reform." *Journal of the American Medical Association*, 265(19): 2532-2536.

Fein, R. (1991). "The Health Security Partnership: a Federal-State Universal Insurance and Cost-Containment Program." *Journal of the American Medical Association*, 265(19): 2555-2558.

Fraker, T., Moffitt. R., and Wolf, D. (1985). "Effective Tax Rates in the AFDC Program." *Journal of Human Resources*, 20(2): 251-63.

Fuchs, V. R. (1991). "National Health Insurance Revisited." *Health Affairs*, 10(4): 7-17.

Gabel G. et al (1989). "Employer-Sponsored Health Insurance in America." *Health Affairs*, Summer: 116-128.

Gallaway, L. E. (1966). "Negative Income Rates and the Elimination of Poverty." *National Tax Journal*, 19: 298-307.

Garfinkel, I. (1992). *Assuring Child Support: An Extension of Social Security*. New York, NY: Russell Sage Foundation.

Garfinkel, I. (1982). *Income-tested Transfer Programs: The Case For and Against* (ed.). New York, NY: Academy Press.

Garfinkel, I. (1978). Welfare Reform (pp. 80-95). *The Social Welfare Forum*. New York, NY: Columbia University Press.

Garfinkel, I. (1974). Income Maintenance Programs and Work Effort: A Review (pp. 1-13), *In Studies in Public Welfare* (Paper No.13). Washington, DC: U.S. Government Printing Office.

Garfinkel, I. (1968). "Negative Income Tax and Children's Allowance Programs: A Comparison." *Social Work*, October: 33-39.

Garfinkel, I. & Haveman, R. (1982). *Income Transfer Policy in the United States: A Review and Assessment* (DP #701-82). Madison, WI: University of Wisconsin-Madison, Institute for Research on Poverty.

Garfinkel, I. & Haveman, R. (1974). "Earnings Capacity and the Target Efficiency of Alternative Transfer Programs." *American Economic Review*, 64(2): 196-204.

Garfinkel, I., & Klawitter, M. M. (1990). "The Effect of Routine Income Withholding of Child Support Collections." *Journal of Policy Analysis and Management*, 9(2): 155-177.

Garfinkel, I., Manski, C. F. & Michalopoulos, C. (1992). Micro Experiments and Macro Effects, In C. F. Manski and I. Garfinkel (Eds.), *Evaluating Welfare and Training Programs*. Cambridge, MA: Harvard University Press.

Garfinkel, I., McLanahan, S. S., & Robins, P. K. (1992) (Eds.). *Child Support Assurance: Design Issues, Expected Impacts, and Political Barriers As Seen From Wisconsin*. Washington, DC: Urban Institute Press.

Garfinkel, I., & McLanahan, S. S. (1986). *Single Mothers and Their Children: A New American Dilemma*. Washington, DC: The Urban Institute Press.

Garfinkel, I., & Melli, M. (1982). *Child Support: Weakness of the Old and Features of a Proposed New System* (Special Report Series,

SR-32A). Madison, WI: University of Wisconsin-Madison, Institute for Research on Poverty.

Garfinkel, I., Oellerich, D. (1989). "Noncustodial Father's Ability to Pay Child Support." *Demography*, 26(2): 219-233

Garfinkel, I., Oellerich, D., & Robins, P. K. (1990). *Child Support Guidelines: Will They Make a Difference?* (DP #912-90). Madison, WI: University of Wisconsin-Madison, Institute for Research on Poverty.

Garfinkel, I., Robins, P. K., Wong, P., & Meyer, D. R. (1990). "The Wisconsin Child Support Assurance System: Estimated Effects on Poverty, Labor Supply, Caseloads, and Costs." *Journal of Human Resources*, 25(1): 1-31.

Ginzberg, E. & Ostow, M. (1991). "Beyond Universal Health Insurance to Effective Health Care." *Journal of the American Medical Association*, 265(19): 2559-2562.

Goldberger, A. S. (1967). Functional Form and Utility: A Review of Consumer Demand Theory (Systems Formulation, Methodology, and Policy Workshop Paper 6703). Madison, WI: University of Wisconsin-Madison, Social Systems Research Institute.

Gornick, M. et al. (1985). "Twenty Years of Medicare and Medicaid: Covered Populations, Use of Benefits, and Program Expenditures." *Health Care Financing Review*, Annual Supplement: 13-59.

Graham, J. W., & Beller, A. H. (1989). "The Effect of Child Support Payments on the Labor Supply of Female Family Heads." *Journal of Human Resources*, 24(4): 664-688.

Green, C. (1967). *Negative Taxes and the Poverty Problem.* Washington, DC: Brookings Institution.

Green, C., & Lampman, R. (1967). "Schemes for Transferring Income to the Poor." *Industrial Relations*, 6: 121-137.

Green Book (1989-91), *Overview of Entitlement Programs* (Committee on Ways and Means U.S. House of Representatives). Washington, DC: U.S. Government Printing Office.

Grumbach, K., Bodenheimer, T., Himmelstein, D. U., & Woolhandler, S. (1991). "Liberal Benefits, Conservative Spending: The Physicians for a National Health Program Proposal." *Journal of the American Medical Association*, 265(19): 2549-2554.

Hausman, J. (1985). "The Econometrics of Non-Linear Budget Sets." *Econometrica*, 53(November): 1255-82.

Haveman, R. H. (1987). *Poverty Policy and Poverty Research*, 1965-1980, Madison, WI: University of Wisconsin-Madison Press.

Health Insurance Association of American (1990, Oct.) *Health Care Financing for All Americans* (advertizing material). Washington, DC.

Helms. J., Newhouse, J. P., & Phelps C. E. (1978). "Copayments and Demand for Medical Care: the California Medicaid Experience." *Bell Journal of Economics*, 19(Spring): 192-208.

Himmelstein, D. U. & Woolhandler, S. A. (1989). "A National Health Program for the United States: A Physicians' Proposal." *New England Journal of Medicine*, 320: 102-108.

Hoagland, G. W. (1980, April). The Effectiveness of Current Transfer Programs in Reducing Poverty. Paper Presented at Conference on Welfare Reform, Goals and Realities. Vermont: Middlebury.

Hofferth, S. (1985). "Updating Children's Life Course." *Journal of Marriage and Family*. 47: 93-116.

Holahan, J., Moon, M., Welch, W. P. & Zuckerman, S. (1991). "An American Approach to Health System Reform." *Journal of the American Medical Association*, 265(19): 2537-2531.

Holahan, J. & Zedlewski, S. (1992). "Who Pays for Health Care in the United States? Implications for Health System Reform." *Inquiry*, 29(2): 231-248.

Holahan, J. & Zedlewski, S. (1991). "Expanding Medicaid to Cover Uninsured Americans." *Health Affairs*, Spring: 45-61.

Hoshino, G. (1969). "Britain's Debate on Universal or Selective Social Services: Lessons for America." *Social Service Review*, 43(3): 245-258.

Huston, A. C. (1991) (ed.). *Children in Poverty*. Cambridge, MA: Cambridge University Press.

Jenkins, S. (1991). Recent Trends in UK Income Inequality, In D. Slottje (Ed.), *Research on Economic Inequality*. Greenwich, CT: JAI Press.

Johnson, T. R. & Pencavel, J.H. (1984). "Dynamic Hours of Work Functions for Husbands, Wives, and Single Females." *Econometrica*, 52 (March): 363-89.

Jones, S. B. (1992). "Employer-Based Private Health Insurance Needs Structural Reform." *Inquiry*, 29(Summer): 120-127.

Kahn, A. J. & Kamerman, S. B. (1988). *Child Support: From Debt Collection to Social Policy*. Newbury Park, CA: Sage Publications.

Kamerman, S. B. & Kahn, A. J. (1988). *Mathers Alone: Strategies for A Time of Change*. Dover, MA: Auburn House Publication Co.

Katharine, R., et al. (1991). "National Health Expenditures, 1990." *Health Care Financing Review*, 13(1):

Keintz, R. M. (1974). *National Health Insurance and Income Distribution*. Lexington: Lexington Books.

Kesselman, J. R. & Garfinkel, I. (1978). "Professor Friedman, Meet Lady Rhys-Williams: NIT vs CIT." *Journal of Public Economy*, 10: 179-216.

Killingsworth, M. R. (1983). *Labor Supply*. Cambridge, MA: Cambridge University Press.

Kimmel, J. (1992). Health Insurance and the Employment Behavior of Single and Married Mothers. Presented at the January 1993 Winter Econometric Society Meetings.

Kraft, J. & Olsen, E. (1977). The Distribution of Benefits from Public Housing, In F.T. Juster (Ed.), *The Distribution of Economic Well-Being*. Cambridge, MA: Ballinger Publishing Company.

Krasue, H. D. (1981). *Child Support in America: The Legal Perspective*. Charlottesville, VA: Michie Co.

Lerman, R. I. (1989). Child-Support Policies, In P. H. Cottingham, & D. T. Ellwood (Eds.), *Welfare Policy for the 1990s* (pp. 219-246). Cambridge, MA: Harvard University Press.

Levitan, S. A. (1990). *Programs in Aid of the Poor* (6th Ed.). Baltimore, MD: The Johns Hopkins Press.

Levitan, S. A. & Shapiro, I. (1987). *Working but Poor: American Contradiction*. Baltimore: The Johns Hopkins University Press.

Lewin, M. E. (1993). Health Care Reform Issues and Strategies: An Overview, In J. A. Meyer & S. S. Carroll (Eds.), *Building Blocks for Change: How Health Care Affects Our Future* (pp. 1-17). Washington, DC: The Economic and Social Research Institute.

Lewis, G. H. & Michel, R. C. (1989) (Eds.). *Microsimulation Techniques for Tax and Transfer Analysis*. Washington, DC: The Urban Institute Press.

Lewit, E. M., Larson, C. S., Gomby, D. S., Shiono, P. H., & Behrman, R. E. (1992). "Medical Care and Children's Health." *The Future of Children*, 2(2): 9-22.

Lidman, R. (1972). "Cost and Distributional Implications of a Credit Income Tax Plan." *Public Policy*, 20(2): 311-334.

Lieberman, J. I. (1986). *Child Support in America*. New Haven, CT: Yale University Press.

Long, S. H. & Marquis, M. S. (1993). "Gaps in Employer Coverage: Lack of Supply Or Lack of Demand?" *Health Affairs*, Supplement: 282-293.

Manning, W. G., Newhouse, J. P., Duan, N., Keeler, E. B., Leibowitz, A., & Marquis, M. S. (1987). "Health Insurance and the Demand for Medical Care: Evidence from a Randomized Experiment." *The American Economic Review*, 77(3): 251-277.

National Commission on Children (1991). *Beyond Rhetoric: A New American Agenda for Children and Families*. Washington, DC: National Commission on Children.

National Commission to Prevent Infant Mortality (1992, March). *Troubling Trends Persist: Short-changing America's Next Generation*. Washington, DC.

Masters, S. & Garfinkel, I. (1977). *Estimating the Labor Supply Effects of Income Maintenance Alternatives*. New York, NY: Academic Press.

McDonald, A. D., McDonald, J. C., Salter, V., & Enterline, P. (1974). "Effects of Quebec Medicare on Physician Consultation for Selected Symptoms." *New England Journal of Medicine*, 291: 649-652.

Mead, L. M. (1986). *Beyond Entitlement: The Social Obligations of Citizenship*. New York: Free Press.

Meyer, J. A. & Carroll, S. S. (Eds.) (1993), *Building Blocks for Change: How Health Care Affects Our Future*. Washington, DC: The Economic and Social Research Institute.

Meyer, D. R., Garfinkel, I., Robins, P. K., & Oellerich, D. (1991a). *The Costs and Effects of A National Child Support Assurance System* (DP #940-91). Madison, WI: University of Wisconsin-Madison, Institute for Research on Poverty.

Meyer, D. R., Phillips, E., & Maritato, N. L. (1991b). "The Effects of Replacing Income Tax Deductions for Children With Children's Allowances." *Journal of Family Issues*, 12(4): 467-491.

Mitchell, Senator G. (1991). *Health America: Affordable Care for All Americans* (S. 1227; U.S. Senate Committee on Labor and Human Resources). Washington, DC: U.S. Government Printing Office.

Moffitt, R. (1992). "Incentive Effects of the U.S. Welfare System: A Review." *Journal of Economic Literature*. 30(March): 1-61.

Moffitt, R. (1986). "The Econometrics of Piecewise-Linear Budget Constraints." *Journal of Business and Economic Statistics*, 4(July): 317-28.

Moffitt, R. and Wolfe, B. (1992). "The Effect of the Medicaid Program on Welfare Participation and Labor Supply." *Review of Economics and Statistics*, 74(4), 615-626.

Monheit, A. C. & Cunningham, P. J. (1992). "Children Without Health Insurance." *The Future of Children*. 2(2): 154-170.

Musgrave, R. A., Heller, P., and Peterson, G. E. (1970). "Cost Effectiveness of Alternative Income Maintenance Schemes." *National Tax Journal*, 23(5): 140-156.

Newhouse, J. P., Manning, W. G., Morris, C. N. & et al. (1981). "Some Interim Results from a Controlled Trial of Cost Sharing in Health Insurance." *New England Journal of Medicine*, 305: 1501-1507.

Nutter, D. O., Helms, C. M., Whitcomb, M. E., & Weston, W. D. (1991). "Restructuring Health Care in the United States: a Proposal for the 1990s." *Journal of the American Medical Association*, 265(19): 2516-2520.

Oberg, C. N. & Polich, C. L. (1988). "Medicaid: Entering the Third Decade." *Health Affairs*, 7(4): 83-96.

Oellerich, D. T. (1984). *The Effects of Potential Child Support Transfers on Wisconsin AFDC Costs, Caseloads and Recipient Well-Being* (SR #35). Madison, WI: University of Wisconsin-Madison, Institute for Research on Poverty.

Oellerich, D. T., Garfinkel, I., & Robins, P. K. (1991). "Private Child Support: Current and Potential Impacts." *Journal of Sociology and Social Welfare*, 18(1): 3-24.

Okun, A. (1975). *Equality and Efficiency: The Big Tradeoff*. Washington, DC: The Brooking Institution.

Orshansky, M. (1968). Who Was Poor in 1966? In E. M. Burns (Ed.), *Children's Allowances and the Economic Welfare of Children* (The Report of a Conference, pp. 19-60). New York, NY: Citizen's Committee for Children of New York, Inc.

Ozawa, M. N. (1971). "Family Allowances for the United States: An Analysis and a Proposal." *Social Work*, 16(4): 72-84.

Pauly, M. V., Danzon, P., Feldstein, P. & Hoff, J. (1991). "A Plan for 'Responsible National Health Insurance.'" *Health Affairs*, 10(1): 5-25.

Congressional Budget Office (1992). Estimated Effects of Child Support Assurance Programs (Unpublished Draft). Washington, DC: Congressional Budget Office.

Rea, S. A. Jr. (1974). Trade-Offs between Alternative Income Maintenance Programs, In U.S. Congress, Joint Economic Committee, *Studies in Public Welfare* (Paper No.13). Washington, DC: U.S. Government Printing Office.

Reddin, M. (1969). "Universality versus Selectivity." *The Political Quarterly*, Jan/March: 12-22.

Reinhardt, U. E. (1990). Bringing Out the Worst in People: The Corrosive Effects of American Health Insurance. Paper prepared for the National Governors' Association Conference on 'Innovative Partnerships for Affordable Health Care.' Washington, DC.

Rhys-Williams, J. (1953). *Taxation and Incentive*, New York, NY: Oxford University Press.

Rice, T. & Thorpe, K. E. (1993). "Income-Related Cost Sharing in Health Insurance." *Health Affairs*, 12(1): 22-39.

Robins, P. K. (1986). "Child Support, Welfare Dependency, and Poverty." *American Economic Review*, 76: 768-788.

Rockefeller IV, Sen. J. D. (1991). "A Call for Action." *Journal of the American Medical Association*, 265(19): 2507-2510.

Rosen, H. S. (1978). "The Measurement of Excess Burden with Explicit Utility Functions." *Journal of Political Economy*, 86: 121-135.

Roybal, E. R. (1991). "The 'US Health Act': Comprehensive Reform for a Caring America." *Journal of the American Medical Association*, 265(19): 2545-2548.

Sadka, E., Garfinkel, I., & Moreland, K. (1982). Income Testing and Social Welfare: An Optimal Tax-Transfer Model, In I. Garfinkel (ed.), *Income-Tested Transfer Programs: The Case for and Against*. NY: Academic Press.

Sardell, A. (1990). "Child Health Policy in the U.S.: The Paradox of Consensus." *Journal of Health Politics, Policy and Law*. 15(2): 271-304.

Sawhill, I. V. (1988). "Poverty in the U.S.: Why Is It So Persistent?" *Journal of Economic Literature*, 26(3): 1073-1119.

Scholz, J. K. (1993). *The Earned Income Tax Credit: Participation, Compliance, and Antipoverty Effectiveness*. (DP #1020-93).

Madison, WI: University of Wisconsin-Madison, Institute for Research on Poverty.

Schorr, A. L. (1966). *Poor Kids*. New York, NY: Basic Books.

Schwartz, E. (1964). "A Way to End the Means Test." *Social Work*, 9(3): 3-12.

Sheils, J. F. & Wolfe, P. R. (1992). "The Role of Private Health Insurance in Children's Health Care." *The Future of Children*. 2(2): 115-133.

Silow-Carroll, S. (1993). A Tax Credit Proposal for Health Care Reform: the Long-Term Impact on Business, Consumers, and the Economy, In J. A. Meyer & S. S. Carroll (Eds.), *Building Blocks for Change: How Health Care Affects Our Future*. Washington, DC: The Economic and Social Research Institute.

Silow-Carroll, S. & Meyer, J. A. (1993). An Employment-Based System with Cost Controls: an Analysis of the Clinton and Mitchell Health Care Proposals, In J. A. Meyer & S. S. Carroll (Eds.), *Building Blocks for Change: How Health Care Affects Our Future*. Washington, DC: The Economic and Social Research Institute.

Smeeding, T. (1988). *The Children in Poverty: Evidence on Poverty and Comparative Income Support Policies in Eight Countries*. Testimony before the Select Committee on Children, Youth, and Families. Washington, DC: U.S. House of Representatives.

Smeeding, T. (1982). *Alternative Methods for Valuing Selected In-Kind Transfer Benefits and Measuring Their Effect on Poverty* (Technical Paper No.50). Washington, DC: Bureau of the Census.

Smeeding, T. & Moon, M. (1980). "Valuing Government Expenditures: The Case of Medical Transfers and Poverty." *Review of Income and Wealth*, 26(Sept): 305-24.

Smeeding, T., Torrey, B., & Rein, M. (1988). Patterns of Income and Poverty: The Economic Status of Children and the Elderly in Eight Countries, In J.L. Palmer et. al (Ed.), *The Vulnerable*. Washington, DC: The Urban Institute Press.

Smolensky, E., Danziger, S., and Gottschalk, P. (1988). The Declining Significance of Age in the United States: Trends in the Well-Being of Children and the Elderly Since 1939, In J.L. Palmer, T. Smeeding, & B. B. Torrey (Eds.), *The Vulnerable*, Washington, DC: The Urban Institute Press.

Smolensky, E., Stiefel, L., Schmundt, M., & Plotnick, R. (1977). Adding In-Kind Transfers to the Personal Income and Outlay Account: Implications for the Size Distribution of Income, In F.T. Juster (Ed.), *The Distribution of Economic Well-Being*. Cambridge, MA: Ballinger Publishing Company.

Sullivan, S. & Fynn, T. (1992). *Reinventing Health Care: The Revolution at Hand*. Washington, DC: National Committee for Quality Health Care.

Sullivan, C. B., Miller, M., Feldman, R., & Dowd, B. (1992). "Employer-Sponsored Health Insurance in 1991." *Health Affairs*, Winter: 172-185.

Swartz, K. & McBride, T. D. (1990). "Spells Without Health Insurance: Distributions of Durations and Their Link to Point-in-Time Estimates of the Uninsured." *Inquiry*, 27(Fall): 281-288.

Theodore, M. (1971). "On Comparing Income Maintenance Alternatives." *The American Political Science Review*, 65(March): 83-96

Thorpe, K. E. (1989). "Costs and Distributional Impacts of Employer Health Insurance Mandates and Medicaid Expansion." *Inquiry*, 26(Fall): 335-344.

Thorpe, K. E. & Siegel, J. E. (1989). "Covering the Uninsured: Interactions Among Public and Private Sector Strategies." *Journal of the American Medical Association*, 262(15): 2114-2118.

Tobin, J. (1967). "Is a Negative Income Tax Practical?" *The Yale Law Journal*, 77: 1-27.

Tobin, J. (1966). "The Case for an Income Guarantee." *The Public Interest*, 4: 31-41.

Todd, J. S., Seekins, S. V., Krichbaum, J. A., & Harvey, L. K. (1991). "Health Access America -- Strengthening the US Health Care System." *Journal of the American Medical Association*, 265(19): 2503-2506.

U.S. Bureau of the Census (1992, August). *Measuring the Effect of Benefits and Taxes on Income and Poverty: 1979 to 1991* (Current Population Reports, Consumer Income Series P-60, No. 182-RD). Washington, DC: U.S. Department of Commerce.

U.S. Bureau of the Census (1990, November). *Measuring the Effect of Benefits and Taxes on Income and Poverty: 1987-1988 (Supplemental Data)* (Current Population Reports, Consumer

Income Series P-20, No. 433). Washington, DC: U.S. Department of Commerce.

U.S. Bureau of the Census (1990, June). *Child Support and Alimony: 1989* (Current Population Reports Consumer Income Series P-60, No. 173). Washington, DC: U.S. Department of Commerce.

U.S. Bureau of the Census (1989). *Marital Status and Living Arrangements: March 1988* (Current Population Reports, Population Characteristics Series P-20, No. 433). Washington, DC: U.S. Department of Commerce.

U.S. Bureau of the Census (1991). *Statistical Abstract of the United States 1991* (111th Ed). Washington, DC: U.S. Department of Commerce.

U.S. Bureau of the Census (1987). *Statistical Abstract of the United States: 1988* (108th ed.). Washington, DC: U.S. Government Printing Office.

U.S. Bureau of Labor Statistics (1988). Employer Costs for Employee Compensation -- March, 1988. *News*, June 16.

U.S. Bureau of Labor Statistics (1992). *Health Benefits and the Workforce*. Washington, DC: U.S. Government Printing Office.

U.S. General Accounting Office (1991). *Canadian Health Insurance: Lessons for the United States*. Washington, DC: U.S. Government Printing Office.

Vadakin, J. C. (1968a). *Children, Poverty, and Family Allowances*. New York, NY: Basic Books.

Vadakin, J. C. (1968b). "A Critique of the Guaranteed Annual Income." *Public Interest*, 11: 53-66.

Vadakin, J.C. (1958). *Family Allowances: An Analysis of Their Development and Implications*. Miami, FL: University of Miami Press.

Waldo, D., Sonnefeld, S., McKusick, D. & Arnett, R. (1989). "Health Expenditures by Age Group, 1977 and 1987." *Health Care Financing Review*, 10(4): 111-120.

Webb, R. L., Michel, R. C., & Bergsman, A. B. (1989). The Historical Development of the Transfer Income Model (TRIM2), In G. H. Lewis and R. C. Michel (Eds.), *Microsimulation Techniques for Tax and Transfer Analysis*. Washington, DC: The Urban Institute Press.

Weinberg, D. (1981). "Housing Benefits from the Section 8 Housing Program." *Evaluation Review*, 6(1): 5-24.

Wilensky, G. R. (1970). An Income Transfer Computational Model, in *The President's Commission on Income Maintenance Programs: Technical Studies*. Washington, DC: U.S. Government Printing Office.

Winkler, A. (1989). "The Incentive Effects of Medicaid on Women's Labor Supply." *The Journal of Human Resources*, 26(2): 308-337.

Wolfe, B. & Moffitt, R. (1991). "A New Index to Value In-Kind Benefits." *Review of Income and Wealth*, 37(4): 387-407.

Wong, P. (1988). *The Economic Effects of the Wisconsin Child Support Assurance System: A Simulation Study with a Labor Supply Model*. Unpublished Dissertation, Madison WI: University of Wisconsin-Madison.

Woolhandler. S. & Himmerlstein, D. U. (1991). "The Deteriorating Administrative Efficiency of the U.S. Health Care System." *New England Journal of Medicine*, 324(May 2): 1253-1258.

Zedlewski, S. R., Acs, G. P., & Winterbottom, C. W. (1992). "Play-Or-Pay Employer Mandates: Potential Effects." *Health Affairs*, 11(1): 62-83.

Zedlewski, S., Holahan, J., Blumberg, L. & Winterbottom, C. (1993). The Distributional Effects of Alternative Heath Care Financial Options, In J. A. Meyer & S. S. Carroll (Eds.), *Building Blocks for Change: How Health Care Affects Our Future* (pp. 87-144). Washington, DC: The Economic and Social Research Institute.

Index